THE POCKET
AUSTIN OSMAN SPARE

First Edition, 2020

ISBN: 978-1-951226-03-9

Edited by Jake Dirnberger
Designed and typeset by Nathaniel K. Perkins

Published by Trident Press
940 Pearl St.
Boulder, CO 80302
tridentcafe.com/trident-press

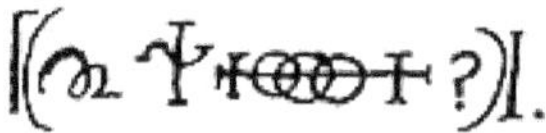

THE POCKET AUSTIN OSMAN SPARE

Edited by Jake Dirnberger

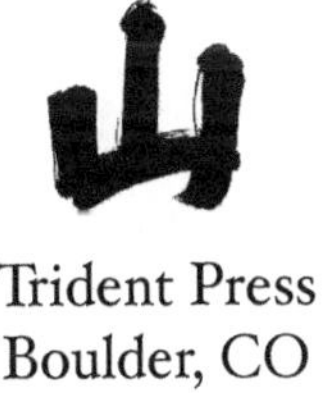

Trident Press
Boulder, CO

Contents

EDITOR'S INTRODUCTION

What does it take to work real, impactful and powerful magic that can change your actual life? Years of study of esoteric tomes? Ancient enchanted relics and tools? Deals with devils and spirits? Circles, brooms, eyes of newt and so on? What if magic is, at its core, none of those? What if all you needed was a pen, some paper, and a little imagination and focus? This was the view of early 20th-century occultist and surrealist artist Austin Osman Spare. Working on the cutting edge of both magic and art, Spare developed a unique synthesis of older ritual magic systems and post-modern, erotic, and surrealist themes. His magic eschews complex formulae and ritual in order to favor creativity, spontaneity, and ecstasy while embracing artistic expression and alternative sexualities. Spare's friend and student, the occult author, Kenneth Grant recalls:

When he was seventeen Spare stayed at the home of the Rev. Robert Hugh Benson, author of *The Necromancers* and other occult novels. They went out for a walk one summer day; a serene and cloudless blue sky shone overhead. It had been fine all day, and Benson was curious to know whether Spare could, in such unlikely circumstances, produce rain by magical means. Spare said he could, proceeded to trace a sigil on the back of a used envelope, and, pausing in his tracks, concentrated all his attention upon it. Within ten minutes small clouds began to appear; they massed at a point immediately above their heads and discharged violently. Both Benson and Spare were drenched to the skin.

How such immediate physical results could issue from just a pen and a scrap of paper will be the focus here, for it shows us Spare's way of conceptualizing reality and mind. Spare developed an occult system that was dense, esoteric and far-reaching, yet utterly simple and straightforward. His writings speak to the nature of reality, human sexuality and evolution, and our mystical and artistic impulses. Perhaps more than any other occult figure, with the possible exception of Aleister Crowley, Spare delivered the practice of magic into the postmodern era, influencing generations of practitioners to follow.

Magic, for Spare, is about bypassing the ordinary mind and harnessing the innate abilities of one's subconscious. "Magic is but one's natural ability to attract without asking," he writes. Indeed, nearly the whole of Spare's methodology boils down to ways to work around the conscious mind. This is most evident in Spare's use of sigils, for which he is perhaps most well known. In sigil work, one decides what object or event they wish to manifest, something like "I desire abundant financial resources," for example. According to one method, one may then eliminate the repeating letters, taking what is left to form the basis of the spell. In this case, "IDESRABUNDTFCLO." Next, one forms an image by scrambling and re-combining the letters, moving around the lines, dots and dashes, simplifying and embellishing the image until they are satisfied. The finished image is called a sigil, a bridge between the conscious and subconscious mind. In this way, the wish is obscured, hidden from the conscious mind's immediate gaze.

"Sigils," says Spare, "are the art of believing; my invention for making belief organic, ergo, true belief." "True belief" for Spare means subconscious belief, what one actually believes even if they don't realize it. A sigil of one's desire is effective because its meaning, the wish encoded in it, is recognizable to the subconscious mind but not to the conscious mind. The magician effectively reprograms his or her subconscious in order to manifest the desired outcome. Once a sigil has been made, it must be activated by pouring the whole of one's awareness into the sigil, then the mind will work unconsciously to manifest the desire in one's life.

Born in London in 1886, Spare became interested in art at a young age. Working first as a draftsman, he eventually accepted a scholarship to the Royal College of Art where his paintings received positive attention. It was also here that he developed an interest in the occult, reading extensively into theosophical and other mystical tracts. Though he eventually dropped out of art school, Spare continued to work as an artist for the remainder of his life. Around the time of his education, Spare claims to have met and trained under a fortune-teller named Mrs. Patterson, a witch so powerful that she could physically manifest her own inner thoughts and impressions. It is from her that Spare claims his magical lineage and inspiration. Though Mrs. Patterson's literal existence is widely doubted, Spare's stories of her speak volumes of his own style of magic: marginalized, egalitarian, feminine, spontaneous, and erotic. He also encountered the renowned British occultist Aleister Crowley around this time, and briefly joined Crowley's magical society A.'.A.'., or *Argenteum Astrum*, though it ultimately proved too rigid and hierarchical for the perennially spontaneous and chaotic young artist. Spare would continue to run in artistic and occult circles for the remainder of his life, authoring a number of his own texts propounding his personal philosophy and magical system. His art was praised for its surreal themes, clear use of lines, and atavistic sexual imagery. Spare died in 1956, relatively impoverished, with only a few close friends and a modest reputation as an artist. Though not widely recognized in his own lifetime for either his artistic or magical works, Austin Osman Spare has had an enduring impact on occult thought, and can be credited more than anyone else as being the father of

"Chaos Magick", a results-oriented bare-bones approach to manifesting one's will which came into prominence in 1970's British punk culture.

Central to Spare's occult philosophy is his concept of *Kia*. This is Spare's concept for a kind of non-dual universal consciousness of which all life partakes. Echoing Lao Tzu's *Tao Te Ching*, Spare writes, "The Kia which can be expressed by conceivable ideas, is not the eternal Kia, which burns up all belief but is the archetype of 'self,' the slave of mortality." The Kia thus stands in contrast to the ordinary self, with its small mind and everyday desires. If it must be expressed in words, Spare tells us, it should be, "the 'Neither-Neither,' the unmodified 'I' in the sensation of omnipresence." In other words, the Kia is beyond words, beyond mind, beyond conceptualization, and yet still has something to do with "self." Spare goes on to say that Kia is also "the primordial sex principle, the idea of pleasure in self-love," and that it is necessary to acheive a state of non-duality uncluttered by thought and desire, called the "death posture." The student of tantra should recognize the annihilation of opposites via mystical union of masculine and feminine principles.

However, Spare goes further than most Hindu and Buddhist tantric sources, equating non-dual mystical states with a self-centered desire for pleasure, often sexual in nature. For Spare, following one's will to pleasure is paramount, and is in fact the only legitimate spiritual path for human beings. In this way, he especially mirrors Aleister Crowley's "Do What Thou Wilt" credo. "Will to pleasure," says Spare, "is the basic function underlying all activity whether conscious or not — and whatsoever the means. Denial of this Self-love is disease—the cause of homicide; the suffering of part-sexualities and small things germinating." Bound up in Spare's pursuit of pleasure-above-all else is a powerful rejection of conventional morality, traditional sexual mores, and self-shame of every type. Indeed, these are part-in-parcel with the small mind that filters out the creative and magical power of Kia. "There is only one sin- suffering. There is only one virtue, the will to self-pleasure." For Spare, selfish pursuit of pleasure is spirituality, but not in the everyday way one might think. Instead the pursuit of pleasure is bound up with the practice of magic: sigil crafting, divination, the evocation and invocation of servitors and spirits, and so on. Pleasure and magical power, for Spare, are mutually-reinforced; the more powerful one's magic, the more avenues and opportunities for pleasure one has, while the more pure pleasure one has, the stronger their connection to Kia grows, and with it their innate magical ability.

That state of "Neither-Neither," from which power, pleasure, and magic can flow, in addition to being a calm meditative state can also be attained through ecstatic means: music, dance, excercise, and, yes, sex. A moment of orgasm, for Spare and other chaos magicians, can be a profound state in which the thinking mind temporarily ceases and Kia can course, potentially making it a powerful instant in which to access the "neither-neither" and work one's magic. Spare tells us:

> This is always secret, communal and periodic; an enforced consummation for almost unlimited wish-fulfillment by lengthy voluntary abstinence, repression and sacrifice until release by mass sexual saturation, for one purpose: the exteriorization of a wish by a great saving and a total spending.

This should recall Crowley's "Love under Will." There must be, for a competent magician, both control and release. Pleasure, for Spare, is both the means and the ends; it is at once a technology the goal of magic. Indeed, the ecstatic and the meditative modes are, in many ways, equal and complementary. Kenneth Grant tells us:

> The New Sexuality, in the sense Spare conceived it, is the sexuality not of positive dualities but of the Great Void, the Negative, the Ain: The Eye of Infinite Potential. The New Sexuality is, simply, the manifestation of non-manifestation...The Mechanics of the New Sexuaility are based upon the dynamics of the Death Posture, a formula evolved by Spare for the purpose of reifying the negative potential in terms of positive power.

In other words, Spare's New Sexuality is *not* a combination of opposites, but a Zen-like *via negativa* that annihilates duality. It is a canceling out which brings one to the verge of profound mystical states from which real power can be wielded, so long as one uses the correct methods. That is why a sigil must enter the mind *whilst* in a state of *Neither-Neither.* The power of Spare's sigil method is that the sigil itself masks what it represents to the mind, and then is also charged while the noise of the conscious mind is at its lowest point. Simply desiring an outcome is ineffective because the conscious mind has no power, and more so can actually manifest the *inverse* desire in the much more agentive subconscious. By both obfuscating the desire and then focusing on it while Kia is at its most powerful, a wish has a path towards real manifestation. Spare writes that, "faith moves no mountains, not till it has removed itself... belief must be organic and sub-conscious." Spare's entire magical technology boils down to the many ways in which one may slip one's desires past the thinking mind and into the universal power of Kia.

Austin Osman Spare, though not well renowned in his life, and even today not widely read outside of certain occult circles, leaves for us a dense and profound legacy to untangle. A truly original thinker, as well as a talented artist, Spare has handed us the keys to many doors through which many are only beginning to peer. Never the leader of a cult-of-personality or a man who claimed the mantle of prophet of the new aeon, Spare encourages us to throw out the outward forms of traditional ceremonial magic and instead to forge our own connections to the universal magical power. His whole system, in fact, is founded on the idea that it is the symbols we craft for ourselves, our own personal arcana, that have the most power. Spare himself made his own sigils, designed his own divinatory cards, and created his own personal spirit-entities (called *servitors* by contemporary chaos magicians). This is a truth that modern day practitioners recognize - that real magic requires a personal and profound connection with the symbols one engages, not a top-down approach wherein one is hammered into a misshapen hole. This in fact may be Spare's most important and impactful contribution to occult thought: They are our own selves, our bodies, our minds, our connection to an infinite wellspring of consciousness and life—Kia—that are the true source of magical power. Collected here are Spare's most important works. Though dense and esoteric, these texts bear repeated study by the serious occultist, for they speak to the very fundamental artistic, erotic, and mystical drives which make us human, and which make real magic possible.

—*Jake Dirnberger, Boulder, CO*

ANATHEMA OF ZOS:
Sermon to the Hypocrite

Hostile to self-torment, the vain excuses called devotion, Zos satisfied the habit by speaking loudly unto his Self. And at one time, returning to familiar consciousness, he was vexed to notice interested hearers—a rabble of involuntary mendicants, pariahs, whoremongers, adulterers, distended bellies, and the prevalent sick—grotesques that obtain in civilisations. His irritation was much, yet still they pestered him, saying: MASTER, WE WOULD LEARN OF THESE THINGS! TEACH US RELIGION! And seeing, with chagrin, the hopeful multitude of Believers, he went down into the Valley of Stys, prejudiced against them as FOLLOWERS. And when he was ennuye, he opened his mouth in derision, saying: O, ye whose future is in other hands! This familiarity is permitted not of thy—but of my impotence. Know me as Zos the

Goatherd, saviour of myself and of those things
I have not yet regretted. Unbidden ye listen'd to
my soliloquy. Endure then my Anathema. Foul
feeders! Slipped, are ye, on your own excrement?
Parasites! Having made the world lousy, imag-
ine ye are of significance to Heaven? Desiring
to learn— think ye to escape hurt in the rape of
your ignorance? For of what I put in, far more
than innocence shall come out! Labouring not
the harvest of my weakness, shall I your mor-
al-fed desires satisfy? I, who enjoy my body with
unweary tread, would rather pack with wolves
than enter your pest-houses. Sensation . . Nutri-
tion . . . Mastication . . . . Procreation . . . ! This is
your blind-worm cycle. Ye have made a curious-
ly bloody world for love in desire. Shall nothing
change except through your accusing diet?

IN THAT YE ARE CANNIBALS, what meat
should I offer? Having eaten of your dead selves
savoured with every filth, ye now raven to glut-
ton of my mind's motion? In your conflict ye
have obtained . . . ? Ye who believe your procre-
ation is ultimate are the sweepings of creation
manifest, returning again to early simplicity to
hunger, to become, and realise— ye are not yet.
Ye have muddled time and ego. Think ye to curb
the semen SENTIMENTALLY? Ye deny sexuality

with tinsel ethics, live by slaughter, pray to great-
er idiots— that all things may be possible to ye
WHO ARE IMPOSSIBLE. For ye desire saviours
useless to pleasure. Verily, far easier for madmen
to enter Heaven than moral Lepers. Of what
difference is Life or Death? Of what difference
is dream or reality? Know ye nothing further
than you own stench? Know ye what ye think
ye know for certain? Fain would I be silent. Yet
too tolerant is this Sun that cometh up to be-
hold me, and my weakness comes of my dissat-
isfaction of you solicit . . . . but be ye damned
before obtaining fresh exuses of me! Cursed are
the resurrectionists! Is there only body and soul?
Is there nothing beyond entity? No purchase be-
yond sense and desire of God than this blasting
and devouring swarm ye are? Oh, ye favoured of
your own excuses, guffaw between bites! Heaven
is indifferent to your salvation or catastrophe.
Your curveless crookedness maketh ye fallow for
a queer fatality! What! I to aid your self-decep-
tion, ameliorate your decaying bodies, preserve
your lamentable apotheosis of self? The sword-
thrust not salve— I bring! Am I your swineherd,
though I shepherd unto goats? My pleasure does
not obtain among vermin with vain ideas— with
hopes and fears of absurd significance. Not yet

Spare   [5]

am I overweary of myself. Not ye shall I palliate abomination, for in ye I behold your parents and the stigmata of foul feeding.

In this ribald intoxication of hypocrisy, this monument of swindlers' littlenesses, where is the mystic symposium, the hierarchy of necromancers that was? Honest was Sodom! YOUR theology is a slime-pit of gibberish become ethics. In YOUR world, where ignorance and deceit constitute felicity, everything ends miserably, besmirched with fratricidal blood. Seekers of salvation? Salvation of your sick digestion; crippled beliefs: Convalescent desires. Your borrowed precepts and prayers, a stench unto all good nostrils! Unworthy of a soul, your metamorphosis is laborious of morbid rebirth to give habitance to the shabby sentiments, the ugly familiarities, the calligraphic pandemonium, a world of abundance acquired of greed. Thus are ye outcasts! Ye habitate dung-heaps; your glorious palaces are hospitals set amid cemeteries. Ye breathe gay-heartedly within this cess-pit? Ye obtain of half-desires, bent persuasions, of threats, of promises made hideous by vituperatious righteousness! Can you realise of Heaven when it exists WITHOUT? Believing without associating ye are spurious and know not the way of virtue. There is no virtue in truth, nor truth in righteousness. Law becomes of desire's necessity. Corrupt is the teacher, for they who speak have only spent words to give. Believe or blaspheme! Do ye not speak from between your thighs? To believe or unbelieve is the question. Verily, if you believe of the least ye needs must thrive all things. Ye are of all things, of all knowledge, and, belike, will you or stupidity to further self-misery! Your wish? Your heaven? I say your desire is women. Your potential desire a brothel. Ah, ye who fear suffering, who among ye has courage to assault the cloudy enemies of creeds, of the stomach's pious hopes? I blaspheme your commandments, to provoke and enjoy your bark, your teeth grinding! Know ye what ye want? What ye ask? Know ye virtue from maniacal muttering? Sin from folly? Desiring a teacher, who among ye are worthy to learn? Brutally shall I teach the gospel of soul-suicide, of contraception, not preservation and procreation. Fools! Ye have made vital the belief the Ego is eternal,, fulfilling a purpose not lost to you. All things become of desire; the legs to the fish; the wings to the reptile. Thus was your soul begotten. Hear, O vermin! MAN HAS WILLED MAN! Your desires shall become flesh, your dreams reality and no fear shall alter it one whit. Hence do I travel ye into the incarnating abortions, the aberratons, the horrors without sex, for ye are worthless to offer Heaven new sexualities. Once in this world I enjoyed laughter, when I remembered the value I gave the contemptible; the significance of my selfish fears; the absurd vanity of my hopes; the sorry righteousness called I.

And YOU? Certainly not befitting are tears of blood, nor laughter of gods. Ye do not even look like MEN but the strange spawn of some forgotten ridicule. Lost among the illusions begat of duality— are these the differentiations ye make for future entity to ride your bestial self? Millions of times have ye had re-birth and many more times will ye again SUFFER existence.

Ye are of things distressed, living down the truths ye made. Loosing only from my overflow, perchance I teach ye to learn of yourselves? In my becoming shall the hungry satisfy of my good and evil? I strive me neither, and confide subsequent to the event. Know my purpose: To be a stranger unto myself, the enemy of truth. Uncertain of what ye believe, belike ye half-desire? But believe ye this, serving your dialectics: Subscribing only to self-love, the outcroppings of my hatred now speak. Further, to ventilate my own health, I scoff at your puerile dignitaries' absurd moral clothes and ovine faith in a fortuitous and gluttonous future!

Dogs, devouring your own vomit! Cursed are ye all! Throwbacks, adulterers, sycophants, corpse devourers, pilferers and medicine swallowers! Think ye Heaven is an infirmary? Ye know not pleasure. In your sleep lusts, feeble violence and sickly morale, ye are more contemptible than the beasts ye feed for food. I detest your Mammon. Disease partakes of your wealth. Having acquired, ye know not how to spend.

YE ARE GOOD MURDERERS ONLY.

Empty of cosmos are they who hunger after righteousness. Already are the merciful spent. Extinct are the pure in heart. Governed are the meek and of Heaven earn similar disgust. Your society is a veneered barbarity. Ye are precocious primitives. Where is your success other than through hatred? There is no good understanding in your world, this bloody transition by procreation and butchery. Of necessity ye hate, and love your neighbor by devouring. The prophets are nauseating and should be persecuted. Objects of ridicule, their deeds cannot live through their tenets. Actions are the criterion, then how can ye speak other than lies?

Love is cursed. Your desire is your God and execration. Ye shall be judged or your appetite.

Around me I see your configuration— again a swine from the herd. A repulsive object of charity! The curse is pronounce; for ye are slime and sweat-born, homicidally reared. And again shall your fathers call to the help of women.

Ye vainly labour at a rotten Kingdom of Good and Evil. I say that Heaven is catholic— and none shall enter with susceptibility of either. Cursed are ye who shall be persecuted for MY sake. For I say I am CONVENTION entire, excessively evil, perverted and nowhere good-for ye. Whosoever would be with me is neither much of me nor of himself enough. Zos tired, but loathing his hearers too much, he again reviled them saying: Worm-ridden jackals! Still would ye feast on my vomit? Whosoever follows me becomes his own enemy; for in that day my exigency shall be his ruin. Go labour! Fulfil the disgust of becoming yourself, of discovering your beliefs, and thus acquire virtue. Let your good be accidental; thus escape gratitude and it sorry vainglory, for the wrath of Heaven is heavy on easy self-indulgence. In your desire to create a world, do unto others as you would when sufficiently courageous. To cast aside, not save,

I come. Inexorably towards myself; to smash the law, to make havoc of the charlatans, the quacks, the swankers and brawling salvationists with their word-tawdry phantasmagoria; to disillusion and awaken every fear of your natural, rapacious selves. Living the most contemptible and generating everything beastly, are ye so vain of your excuse to expect other than the worst of your imagining? Honesty is unvoiced! And I warn you to make holocaust of your saints, your excuses: these flatulent bellowings of your ignorance. Only then could I assure your lurking desire-easy remission of your bowdlerised sins. Criminals of folly? Ye but sin against self. There is no sin for those of Heaven's delight. I would ye resist not nor exploit your evil: such is of fear, and somnambulism is born of hypocrisy. In pleasure Heaven shall break every law before this Earth shall pass away. Thus if I possessed, my goodness towards ye would be volcanic.

He who is lawless is free. Necessity and time are conventional phenomena. Without hypocrisy or fear ye could do as ye wish. Whosoever, therefore, shall break the precept or live its transgression shall have relativity of Heaven. For unless your righteousness exist not, ye shall not pleasure freely and creatively. In so much as ye sin against doctrine, so shall your imagination be required in becoming. It has been said without wit: "Thou shalt not kill." Among beasts man lives supremely-on his own kind. Teeth and claws are no longer sufficient accessory to appetite. Is this world's worst reality more vicious than human behaviour? I suggest to your inbred love of moral gesture to unravel the actual from the dream.

Rejoice ye! The law-makers shall have the ugly destiny of becoming subject. Whatsoever is ordained is superseded-to make equilibrium of this consciousness rapport with hypocrisy. Could ye be arbitrary? Belief foreshadows its inversion. Overrun with forgotten desires and struggling truths, ye are their victim in the dying and begetting law. The way of Heaven is a purpose-anterior to and not induced by thought. Desire, other than by the act, shall in no wise obtain: Therefore believe SYMBOLICALLY or with caution. Between men and women having that desire there is no adultery. Spend the large lust and when ye are satiated ye shall pass on to something fresh. In this polite day it has become cleaner to fornicate by the wish than to enact.

Offend not your body no be so stupid as to let your body offend ye. How shall it serve ye to reproach your duality? Let your oath be in earnest; though better to communicate by the living act than by the word. This God—this cockatrice—is a projection of your imbecile apprehensions, your bald grossness and madhouse vanities. Your love is born of fear; but far better to hate than further deception. I would make your way difficult. Give and take of all men indiscriminately. I know your love and hate. Inquire of red diet. Within your stomach is civil war.

Only in Self-love is procreative will. What now! Shall I attempt wisdom by words? Alphabetic truths with legerdemain grammar? There is no spoken truth that is not PAST— more wisely forgotten.

Shall I scrawl slippery paradox with mad calligraphy? Words, mere words! I exist in a wordless world, without yesterday nor to-morrow beyond becoming.

All conceivableness procures of time and space. Hence I spit on your tatterdemalion ethics, mouldering proverbs, priestly inarticulations and delirious pulpit jargon. This alone I give ye as safe commandments in your pestilent schisms.

Better is it to go without than to borrow. Finer far to take than beg. From Puberty till

Death realise "Self" in all. There is no greater virtue than good nourishment. Feed from the udder, and if the milk be Sour, feed on . .. Human nature is the worst possible!

Once I lived among ye. From self-decency now I habitate the waste places, a willing outcast; associate of goats, cleaner far, more honest than men. Within this heterogenousness of difference, reality is hard to realise; evacuation is difficult. These spiritualists are living sepulchres. What has decayed should perish decently. Cursed are they who supplicate. Gods are with ye yet. Therefore let ye who pray acquire this manner: O Self my God, foreign is thy name except in blasphemy, for I am thy iconoclast. I cast thy bread upon the waters, for I myself am meat enough. Hidden in the labyrinth of the Alphabet is my sacred name, the SIGIL of all things unknown. On Earth my kingdom is Eternity of DESIRE. My wish incarnates in the belief and becomes flesh, for, I AM THE LIVING TRUTH. Heaven is ecstacy; my consciousness changing and acquiring association. May I have courage to take from my own superabundance. Let me forget righteousness. Free me of morals. Lead me into temptation of myself, for I am a tottering kingdom of good and evil. May worth be acquired through those things I have pleasured. May my trespass be worthy. Give me the death of my soul. Intoxicate me with self-love. Teach me to sustain its freedom; for I am sufficiently Hell. Let me sin against the small beliefs. AMEN.

Concluding his conjunction, Zos said: Again, O sleep-walkers, beggars and sufferers, born of the stomach; unlucky men to whom happiness is necessary! Ye are insufficient to live alone, not yet mature enough to sin against the law and still desire women. Other than damnation I know no magic to satisfy your wishes; for ye believe one thing, desire another, speak unlike, act differently and obtain the living value. Assuredly inclination towards new faculties springs from this bastardy! Social only to the truths convenient to your courage, yet again beasts shall be planted. Shall I speak of that unique intensity without form? Know ye the ecstasy within? The pleasure between ego and self? At that time of ecstasy there is no thought of others; there is NO THOUGHT. Thither I go and none may lead. Sans women your love is anathema! For me, there is no way but my way. Therefore, go ye your way— none shall lead ye to walk towards yourselves. Let your pleasures be as sunsets, HONEST .. BLOODY ... GROTESQUE!

Was the original purpose the thorough enjoyment of multitudinous self, for ecstasy? These infinite ramifications of consciousness in entity, associating by mouth, sex, and sense! Has the besetting of sex become utter wretchedness, repetition made necessary of your scotomy?

O bloody-mouthed! Shall I again entertain ye with a little understanding? An introspection of cannibalism in the shambles of diet, the variating murder against the ancestral? Is there no food beyond corpse? Your murder and hypocrisy must pass before ye are uplifted to a world where slaughter is unknown. Thus, with a clean mouth, I say unto ye, I live by bread alone. Sleep is competent prayer. All morality is BEASTLY. Alas, there has been a great failure. Man is dead. Only women remain. With tongue in cheek I would say: "Follow me! That ye realise what is hidden in all suffering. I would make your self-mortification voluntary, your wincing courageous." Still will ye be with me? Salutation to all suicides!

With a yawn Zos wearied and fell asleep. In time the stench awoke him—for he had slept amidst the troughs—and he observed that the crowd were no longer with him, that only SWINE remained. And he guffawed and spake thus: "Not yet have I lost relationship and am thereby nearly asphyxiated! Caught up am I in the toils of sentiment, the moral hallucinations within the ebb and flow of hopes and fears? Shall age alone transmute desire? Not yet have I disentangled illusion from reality: for I know not men from swine, dreams from reality; or whether I did speak only unto myself. Neither know I to whom my anathema would be the more impressionable . . . . My insensible soliloquy is eaten as revelation! What I spake with hard strived conceit to increase enterprise brings forth only swinish snorts. Water is not alone in finding its level. I have not me tragedy, no, not in this life! Yet, whether I have spewed their doctrines upon the tables of the Law or into the troughs, at least I have not cast away the flesh of dreams. And turning towards his light, Zos said: This my will, O Thou Glorious Sun. I am weary of my snakes descending, making slush. Farewell antithesis. I have suffered. All is paid. Let me go forth to recreate my sleep.

THE BOOK OF PLEASURE (SELF LOVE):
The Psychology of Ecstasy

DEFINITIONS

The words God, religions, faith, morals, woman, etc. (they being forms of belief), are used as expressing different "means" as controlling and expressing desire: an idea of unity by fear in some form or another which must spell bondage-the imagined limits; extended by science which adds a dearly paid inch to our height: no more.

KIA: The absolute freedom which being free is mighty enough to be "reality" and free at any time: therefore is not potential or manifest (except as it's instant possibility) by ideas of freedom or "means," but by the Ego being free to recieve it, by being free of ideas about it and by not believing. The less said of it (Kia) the less obscure is it. Remember evolution teaches by terrible punishments-that conception is ultimate reality but not ultimate freedom from evolution.

VIRTUE: Pure Art

VICE: Fear, belief, faith, control, science, and the like.

SELF-LOVE: A mental state, mood or condition caused by the emotion of laughter becoming the principle that allows the Ego appreciation or universal association in permitting inclusion before conception.

EXHAUSTION: That state of vacuity brought by exhausting a desire by some means of dissipation when the mood corresponds to the nature of the desire, i.e., when the mind is worried because of the non-fulfilment of such desire and seeks relief. By seizing this mood and living, the resultant vacuity is sensitive to the subtle suggestion of the Sigil.

DIFFERENT RELIGIONS & DOCTRINES AS MEANS TO PLEASURE, FREEDOM, AND POWER.

What is there to believe, but in Self? And Self is the negation of completeness as reality. No man has seen self at any time. We are what we believe and what it implies by a process of time in the conception; creation is caused by this bondage to formula.

Actions are the expressions of ideas bound up in the belief; they being inherent are obscure, their operation indirect, easily they deceive introspection. Fruits of action are two-fold, Heaven or Hell, their Unity or Nothingness (Purgatory or Indifference). In Heaven there is desire for Women. Hell the desire intense. Purgatory is expectation delayed. Indifference but disappointment till recovery. Then verily they are one and the same. The wise pleasure seeker, having realised they are "different degrees of desire" and never desirable, gives up both Virtue and Vice and becomes a Kiaist. Riding the Shark of his desire he crosses the ocean of the dual principle and engages himself in self-love.

Religions are the projection of incapacity, the imaginations of fear, the veneer of superstition, that paradox is truth[1], while ofttimes the ornamentation of imbecility. As a virtue in the Idea to maximize pleasure cheaply, remit your sins and excuse them—is but ceremonial, the expression of puppetry to the governing fear. Yes!

---

1. *That God is always in Heaven or that the Almighty inconceivable emanates its conception or negation—commits suicide, etc.*

What you have ordained in your religiousness, is your very rack, imagined though it be! The prospect is not pleasant; you have taught yourself! It has become inborn and your body is sensitive.

Some praise the idea of Faith. To believe that they are Gods (or anything else) would make them such-proving by all they do, to be full of its non-belief. Better is it to admit incapacity or insignificance, than reinforce it by faith; since the superficial "protects" but does not change the vital. Therefore reject the former for the latter. Their formula is deception and they are deceived, the negation of their purpose. Faith is denial, or the metaphor Idiotcy, hence it always fails. To make their bondage more secure Governments force religion down the throats of their slaves, and it always suceeds; those who escape it are but few, therefore their honour is the greater. When faith perishes, the "Self" shall come into its own. Others less foolish, obscure the memory that God is a conception of themselves, and as much subject to law. Then, this ambition of faith, is it so very desirable? Myself, I have not yet seen a man who is not God already.

Others again, and those who have much knowledge, cannot tell you exactly what "belief" is, or how to believe in what defies natural laws and existing belief. Surely it is not by saying "I believe"; that art has long been lost. They are even more subject to bewilderment and distraction directly they open their mouths full of argument; without power and unhappy unless spreading their own confusion, to gain cogency they must adopt dogma and mannerism that excludes possibility . . . By the illumination of their knowledge they deteriorate in accomplishment. Have we not watched them decay in ration to their expoundings? Verily, man cannot believe by faith or gain, neither can he explain his knowledge unless born of a new law. We being everything, wherefore the necessity of imagining we are not?

Be ye mystic.

Others believe in prayer . . . have not all yet learnt, that to ask is to be denied? Let it be the root of your Gospel. Oh, ye who are living other peoples lives! Unless desire is subconscious, it is not fulfilled, no, not in this life. Then verily sleep is better than prayer. Quiescence is hidden desire, a form of "not asking"; by it the female obtains much from man. Utilize prayer (if you must pray) as a means of exhaustion, and by that you will obtain your desire.

Some do much to show the similarity of different religions; certainly by it I prove the possibility of a fundamental illusion, but that they never realise-or this Ukase they are the mockery, for how much they regret! They suffer more conflict than the unenlightened. With what they can identify their own delusion of fear they call truth. They never see this similarity and the quintessence of religions, their own poverty of imagination and religion's palliation. Better is it to show the essential difference of religions. It is as well to know that various means; is not their object to deceive and govern? Surely then, for the attainment of the transcendental, God and religion should have no place.

Some praise truth so-called, but give it many containers; forgetting its dependence they prove its relationship and paradox, the song of experience and illusion. Paradox is not "truth", but the truth that anything can be true for a time. What supersedes paradox and its implicit ("not necessary"), I will make the foundation of my teaching. Let us determine the deliberative, "the truth" cannot be divided. Self-love only cannot be denied and is Self-love as such when paradoxical, under any condition, hence it alone is truth, without accessories complete.

Others praise ceremonial Magic, and are supposed to suffer much Ecstasy! Our asylums are crowded, the stage is over-run! Is it by symbolizing we become the symbolized? Were I to crown myself King, should I be King? Rather should I be an object of disgust or pity. These Magicians, whose insincerity is their safety, are but the unemployed dandies of the Brothels. Magic is but one's natural ability to attract without asking; ceremony what is unaffected, its doctrine the negation of theirs. I know them well and their creed of learning that teaches the fear of their own light. Vampires, they are as the very lice in attraction. Their practices prove their incapacity, they have no magic to intensify the normal, the joy of a child or healthy person, none to evoke their pleasure or wisdom from themselves. Their methods depending on a morass of the imagination and a chaos of conditions, their knowledge obtained with less decency than the hyena his food, I say they are less free and do not obtain the satisfaction of the meanest among animals. Self condemned in their disgusting fatness, their emptiness of power, without even the magic of personal charm or beauty, they are offensive in their bad taste and mongering for advertisement. The freedom of energy is not obtained by its bondage, great power not by disintegration. Is it not because our energy (or mind stuff) is already over bound and divided, that we are not capable, let alone magical?

Some believe any and every thing is symbolic, and can be transcribed, and explain the occult, but of what they do not know. (Great spiritual truths?) So argument a metaphor, cautiously confusing the obvious which developes the hidden virtue. This unnecessary corpulency, however impressive, is it not disgusting? (The Elephant is exceeding large but extremely powerful, the swine though odious does not breed the contempt of our good taste.) If a man is no hero to his servant, much less can he remain a mystic in the eyes of the curious; similarity educates mimicry. Decorate your meaning, however objectionable (as fact), after you have shown your honesty. Truth, though simple, never needs the argument of confusion for obscurity; its own pure symbolism embraces all possibilities as mystic design. Take your stand in commonsense and you include the truth which cannot lie; no argument has yet prevailed. Perfect proportion suggest no alteration, and what is useless decays.

They reject all the modern symbolism[2] and reach an absurd limit very early. Not counting on change[3] and (at times) the arbitrary nature of symbolism or the chance of a preserved folly, by their adoption of the traditional without a Science, as having reading to the present, their symbolism is chaotic and meaningless. Not knowing the early rendering, they succeed in projecting their own meagreness by this confusion, as explaining the ancient symbols. Children are more wise. This conglomeration of antiquity decayed, collected with the disease of greed-is surely the chance for charity? Forgetting trumpery ideas, learn the best tradition by seeing your own functions and the modern unbiased. Some praise the belief in a moral doctrinal code, which they naturally and continually transgress, and never obtain their purpose. Given the right nature, <u>they succeed fair</u>ly in their own governing, and

2. *All means of locomotion, machinery, governments, institutions, and everything essentially modern, is vital symbolism of the workings of our mind, etc.*

3. *The symbol of justice known to the Romans is not symbolic of Divine, or our justice, at least not necessarily or usually. The vitality is not exactly like water-nor are we trees; more like ourselves, which might incidentally include trees somewhere unlearnt-much more obvious in our workings at present.*

are those most healthy, sane and self-pleased. It may be called the negation of my doctrine, they obtain tolerable satisfaction, whereas mine is complete. Let him tarry here, who is not strong for the great work. In freedom he might be lost. So fledge your wings fearlessly, ye humble ones!

Others say knowledge only is eternal, it is the eternal illusion of learning-the Ukase of learning what we already know. Directly we ask ourselves "how" we induce stupidity; without this conception what is there we could not know and accomplish? Others for concentration, it will not free you, the mind conceiving the law is bondage. Arrived at that, you will want deconcentration. Dissociation from all ideas but one is not release but imaginative fulfilment, or the fury of creation. Others again, that all things are emanations of the Divine Spirit, as rays from the Sun, hence the need of emancipation? Verily, things are of necessity through their conception and belief. Then let us destroy or change conception, and empty the belief.

These and many other doctrines, are declared by me as the perpetuators of sin and illusion. Each and all depending on a muddled implication, obscuring, yet evolved from the duality of the consciousness for their enjoyment.

In fear they would vomit hot blood were they to see the fruits of their actions and pleasures. Thus believing in widely different doctrines, they are of the dual principle, necessary parasites on each other. Like drugs and the surgeon's knife, they only annul or at best remove an effect. They do not change or remove the fundamental cause (the law). "Oh, God, thou art the stagnant environment." All is quackery: these religions whose very existence depend on their failure, are so full of misery and confusion, have only multiplied arguments, as full of argument as they are evil, so crowded with non-essentials, being so barren of any free pleasure in this life or another, I cannot uphold their doctrines. Their criterion for enjoyment-death! Better it were a man renounce them all, and embrace his own invincible purpose. He cannot go further, and this is his only release. By it he may put his pleasure where he will, and find satisfaction.

THE CONSUMER OF RELIGION

Kia, in its Transcendental and Conceivable Manifestation

Of name it has no name, to designate. I call it Kia I dare not claim it as myself. The Kia which can be expressed by conceivable ideas, is not the eternal Kia, which burns up all belief but is the archetype of "self," the slavery of mortality. Endeavouring to describe "it," I write what may be but not usually-called the "book of lies.[4]" The unorthodox of the originable-a volant "sight," that conveys somehow by the incidental, that truth is somewhere. The Kia which can be vaguely expressed in words is the "Neither-Neither," the unmodified "I" in the sensation of omnipresence, the illumination symbolically transcribed in the sacred alphabet, and of which I am about to write. Its emanation is its own intensity, but not necessariness, it has and ever will exist, the virgin quantum-by its exuberance we have gained existence. Who dare say where, why and how it is related? By the labour of time the doubter inhabits his limit. Not related to, but permitting all things, it eludes conception, yet is the quintessence of conception as permeating pleasure in meaning. Anterior to Heaven and Earth, in its aspect that transcends these, but not intelligence, it may be regarded as the primordial sexual principle, the idea of pleasure in self-love. Only he who has attained the death

4. *About this "Self"; all conception is the dual principle, the law which is its conception.*

posture can apprehend this new sexuality, and its almighty love satisfied. He that is ever servile to belief, clogged by desire, is identified with such and can see but its infinite ramifications in dissatisfaction[5]. The progenitor of itself and all things, but resembling nothing, this sexuality in its early simplicity, embodies the everlasting. Time has not changed it, hence I call it new. This ancestral sex principle, and the idea of self, are one and the same, this sameness its exaction and infinite possibilities, the early duality, the mystery of mysteries,the Sphinx at the gates of all spirituality. All conceivable ideas begin and end as light in its emotion, the ecstasy which the creation of the idea of self induces. The idea is unity by the formula of self, its necessary reality as continuity, the question of all things, all this universe visible and invisible has come out of it. As unity conceived duality, it begot trinity, begot tetragrammaton. Duality being unity, is time, the complex of conception, the eternal refluctuation to the primeval reality in freedom-being trinity of dualities, is the six senses, the five facets of sex-projecting as environment for self-as-

---

5. *The unmodified sex principle refracted through the dual principle emanates the infinite variety of emotions or sexualities, which may be called its ramifications.*

similation in denial, as a complete sexuality. Being tetragrammaton of dualities is twelvefold by arrangement, the human complex, and may be called the twelve commandments of the believer. It imagines the eternal decimal, its multiplicity embracing eternity, from which spring the manifold forms, which constitute existence. Vitalized by the breath of self-love, life is conscious of one. Self being its opposing force, is alternately conflict, harmony, life and death. These four principles are one and the same-the conception considered as the complete "self" or consciousness-hence they may be blended into unity and Symbolized. One form made by two, that is three-fold and having four directions.

The Transcendental Law, the Law and Testament of the "New"

The law of Kia is its own arbiter, beyond necessitation, who can grasp the nameless Kia? Obvious but unintelligible, without form, its design most excellent. Its wish is its superabundance, who can assert its mysterious purpose? By our knowledge it becomes more obscure, more remote, and our faith-opacity. Without attribute, I know not its name. How free it is, it has no need of sovereignty! (Kingdoms are their own despoilers.) Without lineage, who dare claim relationship? Without virtue, how pleasing in its moral self-love! How mighty is it, in its assertion of "Need not be-Does not matter"! Self-love in complete perspective, serves its own invincible purpose of ecstasy. Supreme bliss simulating opposition is its balance. It suffers no hurt, neither does it labour. Is it not self-attracting and independent? Assuredly we cannot call it balance. Could we but imitate its law, all creation without command would unite and serve our purpose in pleasure and harmony. Kia transcending conception, is unchanging and inexhaustible, there is no need of illumination to see it. If we open our mouths to speak of it, it is not of it but of our duality, mighty though it be in its early simplicity! Kia without conceiving, produces its rendezvous as the fulness of creation. Without assertion the mightiest energy, without smallness it may appear the least among things. Its possession ours without asking, its being free, the only thing that is free. Without distinction, it has no favourites, but nourishes itself. In fear all creation pays homage-but does not extol its moral, so everything perishes unbeautifully. We endow ourselves with the power we concieve of it, and it acts as master[6], never the cause of emancipation. Thus for ever from "self" do I fashion the Kia, without likeness, but which may be regarded as the truth. From this consultation is the bondage made, not by intelligence shall we be free. The law of Kia is its ever original purpose, undetermined, without change the emanations, through our conception they materialize and are of that duality, man takes this law from this refraction, his ideas-reality. With what does he balance his ecstasy? Measure for measure by intense pain, sorrow, and miseries. With what his rebellion? Of necessity slavery! Duality is the law, realization by suffering, relates and opposes by units of time. Ecstasy for any length of time is difficult to obtain, and laboured heavily for. Various degrees of misery alternating with gusts of pleasure and emotions less anxious, would seem the condition of consciousness and existence. Duality in some form or another is <u>consciousness as</u> existence. It is the illusion of

6. *By scores of incarnations, our eventual "self" is derived from the attributes with which we endow our God, the abstract Ego or conceptive principle. All conception is a denial of the Kia, hence we are its opposition, our own evil. The offspring of ourselves, we are the conflict of what we deny and assert of the Kia. It would seem as though we cannot be too careful in our choice, for it determines the body we inhabit.*

time, size, entity, etc.-the world's limit. The dual principle is the quintessence of all experience, no ramification has enlarged its early simplicity, but is only its repetition, modification or complexity, never is its evolution complete. It cannot go further than the experience of self-so returns and unites again and again, ever an anti-climax. For ever retrogressing to its original simplicity by infinite complication is its evolution. No man shall understand "Why" by its workings. Know it as the illusion that embraces the learning of all existence. The most aged one who grows no wiser, it may be regarded as the mother of all things. Therefore believe all experience to be illusion, and the law of duality. As space pervades an object both in and out, similarly within and beyond this ever-changing cosmos, there is this secondless principle.

SOLILOQUY ON GOD-HEAD

Who ever Thought Thus?

Something is causing Pain and something energizes the Agony: may it not be caused through the latent Idea of Supreme Bliss? And this eternal expectation, this amassing of ornament on decay, this ever-abiding thought- is coincidental with the vanity preceding death? O, squalid thought from the most morbid spleen how can I devour thee and save my Soul? Ever did it answer back-"Pay homage where due: the Physician is the Lord of existence!" This superstition of medicine-is it not the essence of cowardice, the agent of Death?

Strange no one remembers being dead? Have you ever seen the Sun?-If you have then you have seen nothing dead-in spite of you different belief! Which is the more dead "you" or this corpse? Which of you has the greater degree of consciousness? Judging by expression alone-which of you appears enjoying Life most? May not this "belief" in death be the "will" that attempts "death" for your satisfaction, but can give you no more than sleep, decay, change-hell? This constant somnambulism is "the unsatisfactory."

You disbelieve in Ghosts and God-because you have not seen them? What! You have never seen the mocking ghosts of your beliefs?-the Laughing Bedlam of your humility or Mammon-your grotesque Ideas of "Self"? Yea, your very faculties and your most courageous Lies are Gods! Who is the slayer of your Gods-but a God!

There is no proof that you existed before?

What an excuse! No one has returned to tell us? What a damning advocate! You are but what you were-somehow changed? You are the case Prima Facie that you are reincarnated to perhaps anything? "Perhapses" are possible! Can you do differently to what you do? Never shall I tire of asserting that you constantly do differently!

What is the "ugliness" that offends? Is it the vague knowledge that you will have to change your mind-that you are germinating what you contain? You are always remembering what you forgot; to-day may be the day of reckoning-of believing by force what you disbelieved? Now if to-day is yesterday in all but appearances-then to-morrow also is to-day- the day of decay! Daily is this universe destroyed, that is why you are conscious! There is no Life and Death? Such ideas should be less than comic.

There is no Duality?
You are conscious of the gay Butterfly you observe and are conscious of being "You": the Butterfly is conscious of being "itself," and as such, it is a consciousness as good as and the same as yours, i.e., of you being "you." There-fore this consciousness of "you" that you both feel is the same "you"? Ergo, you are one and

the same-the mystery of mysteries and the most simple thing in the world to understand! How could you be conscious of what you are not? But you might believe differently? So, if you hurt the Butterfly you hurt yourself, but your belief that you don't hurt yourself protects you from hurt-for a time! Belief gets tired and you are miserably hurt! Do what you will-belief is ever its own inconsistency. Desire contains everything, hence you must believe in everything-if you believe at all! Belief seems to exclude commonsense.

There is no doubt about it-this consciousness of "Thee" and "Me" is the unwelcome but ever ready torturer-yet it "need not be so" in any sense! Is it not a matter of Fear? You are fearsome of entering a den of Tigers? (And I assure you it is a matter of righteousness-(inborn or cultured)-whether you enter voluntarily or are chucked in, and whether you come out alive or not!) Yet daily you fearlessly enter dens inhabited by more terrible creatures than Tigers and you come out unharmed-why?

The Allegory

Great scientists are finding out the death-dealing properties of the microbes they discover we breathe, and which according to their canons should destroy; we should be already dead? Have faith! The canons of science are quite correct, they do not disappoint the doubt! Our greater familiarity-"this impulse to knowledge" will certainly bring us the disease and death they give! And also give us in compensation their powers of destruction! For the destruction of whom? Things will be squared! Is this the value of the will? This "will to power"-how life preserving! How furthering of discriminate selection! How pleasing! Most noble explorers! O, you scientists-go on discovering the Bottomless Pit! When you are sodden with science-the lightning will thunder out the murder? New hope will be born? New creatures for the circus? (The conception of) God-head must ever evolve its inertia for transmutation to its very opposite-because it contains it!

The master must be the painful learner of his stupidity?

The idea of God ever means the forgetfulness of supremacy and Godliness. So must be supplanted by fear, eh?

There is no Atheist, no one is free from auto-biography, there is no fearless pleasurist?

The conception is the absence of its indisputable reality within! When the conception is memorial in forgetfulness-it may be the chance of its reality for you?? When the prayer-(you are always praying) has transmuted to its Blasphemy-you are attractive enough to be heard-your desire is gratified! What a somersault of humility!

Whether God is projected as master by fear or as the dweller within by love Gods we are all the time, that is why divinity is always potential. Its constant generation, the eternal delay-is life. This envy of the Master or Creator-the ultimate hope to follow in manner is also existence and the forfeiture of "Life!"

There is no scientific fact, it ever implies its opposite as equal fact, this is the "fact." Then why trouble to prove anything a fact? This vain hope to prove finality is death itself, so why humbug the "Desire"? You have proved (by mathematics!) the sun to be so many millions of miles away from you-you will now improve its efficiency! Nature-that impulse to the antitheses of your truths, will early prove (by mathematics and whenever you like!) that the Sun does not exist at all! Or if you wish-it will prove conclusively that the Sun is millions of millions of miles further away or millions of miles nearer than you once thought! Most extraordinary thinker! These facts and many others are already know to the butterfly, the lice, the insects-and perhaps yourself? Whose senses are the more true-yours or the house-fly's? You will eventually adopt their vision-their thoughts and wisdom-you were such once? You are such now but have not awakened them-you will be such again in power! Wondrous progress! Most meritorious accomplishments! Most merciless! Progress should be closely examined and what you have gained by the convenience of science.

A thought for perspective-you are always what you most wish-the prospective! Your desire is to live according to your desire, and this you are always realizing! Most noble sentiment!-you are "it" already-"the satisfied"-"the desireless"-"the real thing"! You are drunk with it.

There is no illusion but consciousness! This consciousness is ever the smiling monument commemorating "Whether you ever really enjoyed Life"!

The God of the "Will" is the command to obey, its Justice everyone fears it is a Sword-your desert for obedience! "Will" is the command to believe, your will is what you have believed actively willing the belief for you! You think when "it" wishes! "Will" is complication, the means of a means. Call this will free or not-beyond will and belief is Self-love. I know of no better name. It is free to believe what it desires. You are free to believe in nothing related to belief. The "Truth" is not difficult to understand! The truth has no will-will has no truth! Truth is "will" never believed-it has no truth! "Could be"-is the immediate certainty! This haunting Sphinx teaches us the value of the "will to anything"? Then there is no graver risk than Absolute Knowledge-if little is dangerous-what about Omniscience? The Almighty power has no accessories!

Science is the accursed doubt of the possible, yea, of what does exist! You cannot conceive an impossibility, nothing is impossible, you are the impossible! Doubt is delay-time-but how it punishes! Nothing is more true than anything else! What are you not-you ever answered truthfully?

You tyrannise over yourself, so constantly forget what you remember; you resist sense objects and show resistance to the faculties by believing or not. These faculties are as numerous as the atoms you have not yet seen, and they are as endless as the number one-they come into life at will. You adopt a few at a time- knowledge you speak through them- did you but understand your grammar those you disown speak louder than your words! I would not believe the wisdom of the Almighty.

Belief is ever its own tempter to believe differently; you cannot believe freedom but you may be freed from belief? Neither can you believe the "Truth" but you need not compromise yourself. The way of Life is not by "means"-these doctrines-my doctrines even though they allow the self-appointed devotee to emulate my realization- may I ever blush! The man of sorrows is the Teacher! I have taught- would I teach myself or thee again? Not for a gift from Heaven! Mastership equals learning- equals constant unlearning! Almighty is he who has not learnt and mighty is the babe- it has only the power of assimilating!

The most solecistical of fools now asks-"how can we escape the inevitable evolutions of conception-as all is ever conceiving"? My answer shall permit all means, all men, all conditions. Listen, O, God that art, yet would be God. When the mind is nonplussed- capability to attempt the impossible becomes known; by that most simple state of "Neither-Neither" the Ego becomes the Silent Watcher and knows about it all! The "Why" and "How" of desire is contained within the mystic state of "Neither-Neither" and common-sense proves it is the milk state, most nutritious! Clownish that I am- yet all my ideas have come out of it (and, my friend, all yours), but ever have I been a sluggard- an old sinner who would see others almighty before himself.

THE DEATH POSTURE

Ideas of Self in conflict cannot be slain, by resistance they are a reality- no Death or cunning has overcome them but is their reinforcement of energy. The dead are born again and again lie in the womb of conscience. By allowing maturity is to predicate decay when by non-resistance is retrogression to early simplicity and the passage to the original and unity without idea. From that idea is the formula of non-resistance germinating "Does not matter- please yourself."

The conception of "I am not" must of necessity follow the conception of "I am," because of its grammar, as surely in this world of sorrow night follows day. The recognition of pain as such, implies the idea of pleasure, and so with all ideas. By this duality, let him remember to laugh at all times, recognize all things, resist nothing;

then there is no conflict, incompatibility or compulsion as such.

Transgressing Conception by a Lucid Symbolism

Man implies Woman, I transcend these by the Hermaphrodite, this again implies a Eunuch[7]; all these conditions I transcend by a "Neither" principle, yet although a "Neither" is vague, the fact of conceiving it proves its palpability, and again implies a different "Neither.[8]"

But the "Neither-Neither" principle of those two, is the state where the mind has passed beyond conception, it cannot be balanced, since it implies only itself. The "I" principle has reached the "Does not matter- need not be" state, and is not related to form. Save and beyond it, there is no other, therefore it alone is complete and eternal. Indestructible, it has power to destroy-therefore it alone is true freedom and existence. Through it comes immunity from all sorrow, therefore the spirit is ecstasy. Renouncing ev-

7. *Sex-less.*

8. *They being dual have analogy to certain early sex principles in nature. They are carried further in the sacred alphabet, being too abstruse to explain by orthodox words and grammar.*

erything by the means shown, take shelter in it. Surely it is the abode of Kia? This having once been (even Symbolically) reached, is our unconditional release from duality and time- believe this to be true. The belief free from all ideas but pleasure, the Karma through law (displeasure) speedily exhausts itself. In that moment beyond time, a new law can become incarnate, without the payment of sorow, every wish gratified, he[9] having become the gratifier by his law. The new law shall be the arcana of the mystic unbalanced "Does not mattter- need not be," there is no necessitation, "please yourself" is its creed.[10]

In that day there can be deliberation. Without subjection, what youwish to believe can be true. "He[11]" is pleased by this imitation, the truth revealed to me by all systems of government but is himself ungoverned; Kia, the supreme bliss. This the glorious Science of pleasing one's self by a new agreement, the art of Self-love by recognition, the Psychology of ecstasy by non-resistance.

---

9. *The Ego.*

10. *The belief ever striving for denial- fulness by multiplication, is kept free by retention in this.*

11. *"He", the Ego, now becomes the "Absolute."*

[48]

The Ritual and Doctrine

Lying on your back lazily, the body express-
ing the condition of yawning, suspiring while
conceiving by smiling, that is the idea of the pos-
ture. Forgetting time with those things which
were essential-reflecting their meaninglessness,
the moment is beyond time and its virtue has
happened.

Standing on tip-toe, with the arms rigid,
bound behind by the hands, clasped and stran-
ing the utmost, the neck streched- breathing
deeply and spasmodically, till giddy and sensa-
tion comes in gusts, gives exhaustion and capac-
ity for the former.

Gazing at your reflection till it is blurred
and you know not the gazer, close your eyes (this
usually happens involuntarily) and visualize. The
light (always an X in curious evolutions) that is
seen should be held on to, never letting go, till
the effort is forgotten, this gives a feeling of im-
mensity (which sees a small form), whose limit
you cannot reach. This should be practised be-
fore experiencing the foregoing. The emotion
that is felt is the knowledge which tells you why.

The death posture is its inevitability accel-
erated, through it we escape our unending de-
lay by attachment, the Ego is swept up as a leaf

in a fierce gale- in the fleetness of the indeter-
minable, that which is always about to happen
becomes its truth. Things that are self-evident
are no longer obscure, as by his own will he
pleases, know this as the negation of all faith
by living it, the end of the duality of the con-
sciousness. Of belief, a positive death state, all
else as sleep, a negative state. It is the dead body
of all we believe, and shall awake a dead corpse.
The Ego in subjection to law, seeks inertion in
sleep and death. Know the death posture and
its reality in annihilation of law- the ascension
from duality. In that day of tearless lamenta-
tion the universe shall be reduced to ashes . . .
but he escapes the judgment! And what of "I,"
most unfortunate man! In that freedom there is
no necessitation, what dare I say more? Rath-
er would I commit much sin than compromise
myself. There are many preliminary exercises,
as innumerable as sins, futile of themselves but
designative of the ultimate means. The death
posture in the reduction of all conception (sin)
to the "Neither-Neither" till the desire is con-
tentment by pleasing yourself. By this and by no
other are the inertia of belief; the restoration of
the new sexuality and the ever original self-love
in freedom are attained. The primordial vacuity

(or belief) is not by the exercise of focussing the mind on a negation of all conceivable things, the identity of unity and duality, chaos and uniformity, etc., etc., but by doing it now, not eventually. Percieve, and feel without the necessity of an opposite, but by its relative. Percieve light without shadow by its own colour as contrast, through evoking the emotion of laughter at the time of ecstasy in union, and by practice till that emotion is untiring and subtle. The law or reaction is defeated by inclusion. Were he to enjoy an hundred pleasures at a time, however much his ecstasy, he does not lose, but great increase takes place. Let him practise it daily, accordingly, till he arrives at the centre of desire. He has imitated the great purpose. Like this, all emotions should find equipoise at the time of emanation, till they become one. Thus by hindering belief and semen from conception, they become simple and cosmic. By its illumination there is nothing that cannot be explained. Certainly I find satisfaction in ecstasy. I have now told you a secret of great import, it was known to me in childhood. Even by sedulously striving for a vacuity of belief, one is cosmic enough to dwell in the innermost of others and enjoy them. Among men few know what they really believe or desire, let him begin, who would know, by locating his belief till he sees his will. Existing as dual, they are identical in desire, by their duality there is no control, for will and belief are ever at variance, and each would shape the other to its ends, in the issue neither wins as the joy is a covert of sorrow. Let him unite them.

THE CLOUDY ENEMIES BORN OF STAGNANT SELF-HYPNOTISM

Natural belief is the intuition that compels belief through that which is experienced reacting, and dominating in turns; everything has to associate itself through its definite emotion, stimulated by those in harmony; those discordant, lose cogency and inhibit. So by its own workings belief is limited and determined for you. The majority of our actions can be traced back to a subconscious desire (for freedom) in conflict with habit, an obedience to inherent fatalism which hangs on "good and bad" actions already committed (in past existence) against a preserved morality*[12] and whose reaction gives expression as spontaneity, involuntariness, au-

---

12. *The elemental morality or fear of displeasing.*

[52]

tonomy, the deliberate, etc., as the chance aris-
es. The rest is due to a conflicting traditional
moral doctrine that has become constitutional
(partly adopted to govern and time this reac-
tion). In its origin, an idea of what was then
considered conveniently good and bad . . . To
maximize pleasure by an arbitrary compromise
of abstention and performance of desire feared.
Assimilated by the deceit of its divine origin,
its tenets are reward for obedience, punish-
ment for transgression, both holding good for
all time (this world and another). This moral
code is a dramatised burlesque of the concep-
tive faculty, but is never so perfect or simple in
that it allows latitude for change in any sense,
so becomes dissociated from evolution, etc; and
this divorce loses any utility and of necessity for
its own preservation and the sympathy desired,
evolves contradictions or a complication to give
relationship. Transgressing its commandments,
dishonesty shows us its iniquity, for our justifi-
cation; or simultaneously we create an excuse or
reason for the sin by a distortion of the moral
code, that allows some incongruity. (Usually re-
taining a few unforgivable sins- and an unwritten
law.) This negative confession is a feigned ratio-
nalism that allows adventitious excuses... a pro-

cess of self-deception to satisfy and summarily persuade yourself of righteousness. What one among us has any excuse but self-love? We do not create or confess a morality that is convenient, that lends itself to growth, and remains simple, that allows transgression without excuse or punishment. It would be wise and common-sense to do so, whatever the state of affairs in your mind. Nature eventually denies that which it affirms: Through permanent association with the same moral code we help desire to transgress. Desire of those things denied, the more you restrict the more you sin, but desire equally desires preservation of moral instinct, so desire is its own conflict (and weakly enough). Have no fear, the Bull of earth has long had nothing to do with your unclean conscience, your stagnant ideas of morality. The microbe alone would seem without fear!

The Complexity of the Belief (Know Thyself)

The nature of belief equals all possibilities ultimately true by identification through culture to an idea of time, so what is not timely is not true, and what is not true, prognostication. Thought of one thing, implies the possibility of another idea as contradicting but not dissociated, belief is to make "one" more convincing. The condition of belief is the denial or limit imposed on the capability of the vitality. To believe at all as such is a concentration and schooling to exclude the implied by adopting a hypothesis or faith that reflects non-worryingly or deceitfully rationalizes the rejected. Truth is not the truth of formula.

The centre of belief is love for one's self, projecting environment for fulfilment but allowing its distortion to simulate denial, an ambition to become ulterior to self-desire, but you cannot get further than the centre, so one multiplies (believes) in order to be more unaware of the fundamental. Now this refusal to believe what one believes and exactly as one believes, is the first condition for all those who are in desire in any sense whatsoever; the man who is in love perforce becomes a liar, self-hypnotised by his morbid ornamentation. You know the results... You can only "truly believe" one thing, yet its implexion is essential (as the truth seems to kill[13]), so the imagined goes on for ever. The imagination learns that the idea is its compulsion. To explain the "why" of belief (or of anything else), we must transcend its schism. By

13. *And does kill when feared.*

entire consciousness in how the self loves is the means. As we imitate this law of duality in all our processes of believing, it is not so simple as it seems. Who has transgressed the law of conception? Who has no fear? Yet by this sin, is the sciential of what determines the Schetic. Gracefully compelling or expecting disappointment at the time of desire is the means of locating its deceit, a consciousness that alone gives the chance of inquiry. Beyond it is something arbitrary, the pauser, the ordainer of law, imitating it by "reason" is but damning the consequences. Reason is belief, belief is fear of one's capability, the faith that you are not even all the wonders of creation, let alone the possibility of being the creator. It is delay . . . Belief well earns the terrible hatred of the vitality. Belief is not freedom. Belief creates its necessary experience, progress germinates in retrogression. Consider the reality is somewhere: and your belief may be too small for its habitation. Oh, ye of much faith in God, merge into it by the worship of self! Ah! foolish man, worship the glorious in freedom. When death approaches the faith in God and desire of woman will not save you, what are their use when withering and decay sets in and the body is an object of disgust? And what is the use of

[56]

knowledge and charity when reality is known? Unsheathe the sword of self; ideas of the Almighty should be constantly slain and righteousness should be inquired into.

Whosoever shall study his true nature a little, him does the "self" investigate with his extraordinary conduct. He can compel anything without offending. As the tendency of the most lustful ceases before publicity and death, so do morals and faith before the perfect bliss. A glimpse of the truth is born of purity of love: when the desire is without fear, when it does not desire possession. When the thought is fulfilled by vision. The fire that is all pleasure is loosed at his will, he is attraction, the cynosure of women. When the believing principle is devoid of faith, as sterile of possessing ideas of God - he is indestructible. Only when there is no fear in any form is there realisation of identity with reality (freedom). For them there is no danger in negligence, there being no discrimination. For him who is conscious of the slightest differentiation there is fear. So long as there is perception of self-reproach or conscience, there is pain germinating: there is no freedom. He who believes anything he perceives or imagines, falls into sin. By believing without feeling perturbation, forgetting ideas of external and internal, he regards everything as self, and is the consciousness of non-resistance, has no horizon: he is free. On seeing the star-lit eyes and rosebud mouths, the breasts and loins of beautiful women, you become lovingly attached, but if you fear, consider constantly that they are merely the charred flesh and bones of yourself after the torture. The space between the eternal and "self," is it not a moral doctrine? By unbelieving all one believes and sedulously without anxiety not believing (by the "Neither-Neither" process), the principle becomes simple and cosmic enough to include what you are always desiring, and you are free to believe what was impossible. The desire is so mighty, it asks no permission, and suffers no consequences, but the ecstasy of its possession. Against it nothing can prevail, it burns up, as celluloid cast into the furnace- the old folly of promising things on behalf of an imagined "another." At hand is the freedom of Heaven, the Way, the Truth, and the Light, and none dare say this of himself but by me, in Truth I alone am "Self," my will unconditioned, is magical. Those who have lived much in their nature will in some degree be familiar with such a sensation, poor though it be.

PREFACE TO SELF-LOVE

Let us be honest! Thou art "that," supreme in freedom, most desirable, beyond desire, untouched by the six stupifiers. The sexuality labours, so Death may harvest by desire. The elusive fancies of the senses are dangerous, because of the righteousness you have learned to obey and control them by. Hell-fire burns because you "conceived"; and will cease to hurt when you identify the Ego with all the possibilities of its qualities by believing as the "Neither-Neither" process. You are fire yet you are scorched! Because you have "willed" belief (differently or not makes no difference); the cycle of belief goes on and always obliges, so one day you must believe differently and the fire will no longer hurt- you are saved? There are other means of hurting you?

In that state which is not, there is no consciousness in any sense that thou art "that" (Kia), which is superb, beyond the range of definition: there is no temptation of freedom, "it" was not the cause of evolution. Hence "it" is beyond time, consciousness or unconsciousness, everything or nothingness, etc.; this I know through the "Neither-Neither" which is automatically beyond every conception, ever free in every sense. Perhaps "it" may not be obscure by continual afterthought and vaguely felt through the hand of innocence- but whoever understands such simple meanings? "It" is never perceived, being the imperceptible Ecstasy of the "Neither-Neither"- ever present but hidden by exhaustion through the cycle of Unity. The certainty of consciousness is always the uncertainty of the perceived or experienced in whatever state it may be, the constant doubt spelling fear, pain, decay, and the like- the cause of evolution, the eternal incompletion.

O, desire, listen! In point of virulence spiritual desire is as fatal as the sensuous. Aspiration towards a "supreme" is a network of deadly desires because of cowardice within, ergo, some unsatisfied wisdom awaiting exploitation to suffer its evolutions. There is no final wisdom- there is no final desire. How can anything end? Has to-day ever ended? These things are endlessness!

A person desires things of this world- but where is the difference of desiring the "Supreme Bliss"? Which is the more selfish? Which is nearer you? Which pleases the Creator more? Are you certain of the Creator's will and are you sure of your own desire? Are you the Creator or just yourself, as you fondly imagine your contents?

All these desires, however mighty, you will one day incarnate- yea, photograph. These things already exist- very soon you will have spiritual photographs (unfaked) but not by the camera you use at present. The pioneer is ever the old fool. An afterthought: some spirits are already photographed- the microbes.

Are you ever free of desideratum? Belief is eternal desire!

Desire is its own cruelty, the fettering of the hand to labour in some world unknown; nothing is always dead and no thought dies, the master becomes the slave- the position is alternate; you have long believed this, it is in the flesh of your generations with the most merciless Judge! The scorn of all your reforms or the inversion of your values!

This constant curse and blasphemy- is not the relief more in the knowledge of the nascent unrelenting taskmaster?

Are not our bodies all smeared with its blood? Has not the world ever been bloody? Are not our pleasures but rest to drink the blood of slaughter? O, determined Liars, ye know not yet the lie, it may be Truth!

The Ego is desire, so everything is ultimately desired and undesirable, desire is ever a preliminary forecast of terrible dissatisfaction hidden by its ever-present vainglory. The millenium will come and quickly go. Men will be greater than the Gods they ever conceived- there will be greater dissatisfaction. You are ever what you were but you may be so in a different form!

A person or a nation, however vain or content, falls immediately into unknown and inevitable desire, consuming him little by little through those conditions- any condition!

The mind becomes firm in desire by desire as devotion, but when realized is it then eternally desirable? (or even for a period of a million years). In Heaven shall be fettered thy foot! Therefore remove the conception that desire is pure, or impure, or has completion- remove it by the "Neither-Neither." Even whether the desire is for the exhasustion of desire by the "neither-Neither" or for realization in a wife- it is desire- its unending evolution. Therefore remove desire in any form by the "Neither-Neither." Remove the illusion that there is Spirit and Not-Spirit (this idea has never given beneficial results). Remove all conceptions by the same means.

So long as the notion remains that there is "compulsory bondage" in this World or even in dreams there is such bondage. Remove the conception of Freedom and Bondage in any World or State by meditation on Freedom in Freedom by the "Neither-Neither."

For this we know- Vampirism is quite well proven enough- even by the strong presumption that whenever blood-sucking is done, it is done by Vampire bats apart from the probability of it being done by a divine or human agency!

Therefore Kiaize desire by the "Neither-Neither," the most excellent formula far beyond contentment- the all-embracing vacuum which reduces "all" to common sense and upon which this Universe rests.

Therefore believe nothing in this Book by the "Neither-Neither," and dispel the conception of the "Neither-Neither" by the "Neither-Neither," and belive it is "not-necessary" or the conclusion of pleasing yourself, because it "Need-not-be-Does-not-matter."

One believes this "all the time" as the Truth of "The Will" not the thing believed, since the means to an end mean evolution to endless means.

In that most remarkable simplicity there is no beginning or end of wisdom or of anything, so how can it be related to conception and Intelligence?

SELF-LOVE AS A MORAL DOCTRINE & VIRTUE

The criterion of action, is freedom of movement, timeliness of expression, pleasuring. The value of a moral doctrine is in its freedom for transgression. Simplicity I hold most precious. Are not the most simple things in the world the most perfect, pure, innocent, and their properties the most wonderful? Hence it is the source of wisdom. Wisdom is exactly happiness. In love pleasuring myself necessarily without excuse. Is this not perfection? Actions would appear unfathomable and incomprehensible, did they exhibit conformity to the great purpose. There are few who can attain to this! Who has no shame? Ecstasy in satisfaction is the great purpose. Freedom from the necessity of law, realisation by the very wish, is the ultimate goal. Law depends on two, two is uberty, millions . . . Law is complicated. The second did not agitate, the first did not determine, nor was it compelled or proffered. Chance in sport is not prophecy; by it we have gained proficiency, sufficient to determine... Prepare for the Eternal, revert to simplicity and you are free. What man can give without impulse? Only he who has complete sexuality. The highest goodness is self-nourishment. What are we going to include as self? Perfect charity acquires, hence it benefits all things by not giving. What man can have faith without fear? Only he who has no duty to perform. When faith perishes duty to moral doctrines perishes, we are without sin and endure for ever in all-devouring love. What man can know with certainty? Only he who has effaced the necessity of learning. When teachers fall out, what is the use of learning from them? The wise are not contentious and have no dogma to expound . . . rather are they silent as a new-born babe in feeding. Whatteacher can show the source of wisdom? It is because I know without learning; I know the source and can convey lessons without teaching. Knowledge is but the excrement of experience: experience its own repetition. The true teacher implants no knowledge but shows him his own superabundance. Keeping his vision clear he directs or leads him as a child to the essential. Having shown him the source of wisdom, he retires before gratitude or sentiment sets in, leaving him to fertilize as he wishes. Is not this the way of Heaven? He who trusts to his natural fund of genius, has no knowledge of its extent and accomplishes with ease, but directly he doubts, ignorance obsesses him. Doubt fertilizes in the virgin soil. He is no longer fearless but a coward to difficulties, his very learning is fear. The difference between genius and ignorance is a degree of fear. The beginning of wisdom is fear of forethought the reception of knowledge in learning. Children doubt, and abhor learning. Why, even the affection of courage results in cleverness! The difference between good and evil is a matter of profundity. Which is nearer you, self-love and its immorality or love and morals? Not conscious of desert the compeer of Heaven, and constant happiness in wisdom is the capacity of direction. From self-glorification, from self-exaltation we rise superior to the incapacity of disquieting fear: the ridiculer to destruction of humility in repentance. This "self-love" that does not give but is glad to receive is the genuine opportunity for freedom from covetousness, from the militant amusement of Heaven. He who subordinates animal instincts to reason, quickly loses control. Are not the animals we see in circuses trained by torture? And do not the animals reared in love, slay their master? The wise embraces and nourishes all things, but does not act as master. Only when passions are ruled by foreign environment are they dangers. Control is by leaving things to work out their own salvation- directly we interfere we become identified with and subject to their desire. When the Ego sees self-love- there is peace it becomes the seer. Directly we desire, we have lost all; "we are" what we desire, therefore we never obtain. Desire nothing, and there is nothing that you shall not realise. Desire is for completion, the inherent emotion that it is "all happiness," all wisdom, in constant harmony. But directly we believe, we are liars- and become identified with pain, yet pain and pleasure are one and the same. Therefore believe nothing, and you will have reverted to a simplicity which childhood has not yet attained. The fool asks how? as we must believe in pleasure and pain. Now if we could suffer them simultaneously (pain and pleasure) and hold fast to a principle that ascends, that allows the Ego vibration above them, should we not have reached the ecstasy? Now the belief is the "Ego," yet separates it from Heaven as your body separates you from another's. . . . . Therefore by retaining the belief in the "not necessity" (when conceiving), the Ego is free. The emotion of laughter is exhaustion, the early suffering hence by making this emotion a "mental state" at the time of unity[14] he unites pain and pleasure, suffers them simultaneously and by the "not necessity" of his belief, his conception transcends this world and reaches the absolute ecstasy. There is no place where pain or death can enter.

The idea of God is the primordial sin, all religions are evil. Self-love is its own law, which may be broken with impunity, being the only energy that is not servile, serving its ever-ready purpose. Surely it is all that is left us that has no sin and is free? Verily, it is the only thing we dare be conscious of. He that truly pleases himself is wihout virtue, and shall satisfy all men. Hate, jealousy, murder, etc., are conditions of love, even as virtue, greed, selfishness, suicide, etc., are conditions or not pleasing ones's self. There is no sin more sickening than love, for it is the very essence of covetousness and the mother of all sin, hence it has the most devotees. Self-love only is pure and without a congregation.

14. *Of Sex, indeed of everything.*

[68]

He that entirely loves himself induces self-love only. In this he is inexorable, but does not offend like other men. He is akin to the great purpose, his actions explained for him, good seen of his evil, without knowing, everyone satisfied with his will. Do not Heaven and Earth unite daily in spontaneous homage to this will of self-love? No man can show greater self-love, than by giving up all he believes. Why do I value this self-love before all else? Is it not because I may be free to believe in evil, but have no thought that anything can do me injury? All is self-love, the people of the world, if they only knew, are its devotees. My new law is the great clue to life. If the world could understand this, the rotten fabric discarded, they would diligently follow the way in their own hearts, there would be no further desire for unity. . . . . Try and imagine what that implies.

May the idea of God perish and with it women: have they not both made me appear clownish? Let there be no mistake, purity and innocence is simplicity, happiness is wisdom. What is simple has no duality.

THE DOCTRINE OF
ETERNAL SELF-LOVE

Now self-love is explained. It is the completion of belief. The "self" is the "Neither-Neither," nothing omitted, indissoluble, beyond prepossession; dissociation of conception by its own invincible love is the only true, safe, and free. The desire, will, and belief ceasing to exist as separate. Attraction, repulsion, and control self contained, they become the original unity, inert in pleasure. There is no duality. There is no desire for unity. At that time, it (the dual principle) rests in its unmodified state. The belief no longer subject to conception by conceiving "self" as such by loving. At other times, it[15] creates a centre, becomes its environment, identified with its ramifications, conception created, subjection to law and the insatiable desire for unity, inasmuch as the duality is unity. Servitude

15. *It the "Neither-Neither" emanates tetragrammaton of relatives, the sexes of which are evolved through their cruciform reflection and are elusive to identity. In their XXXX they produce unity XXXXX XXXXX conception. Ego generating by subdivision they embrace eternity, in their manifold ramifications is law.*

to law is the hatred of Heaven. Self-love only is the eternal all pleasing, by meditation on this effulgent self which is mystic joyousness. At that time of bliss, he is punctual to his imagination, in that day what happiness is his! A lusty innocent, beyond sin, without hurt! Balanced by an emotion, a refraction of his ecstasy is all that he is conscious of as external.[16] His vacuity causes double refraction, "He," the self-effulgent lightens in the Ego. Beyond law and the guest at the "Feast of the Supersensualists."[17] He has power over life and death[18]. Save by this, he is not beyond self-reproach, verily he has loosed all the trouble of the world, the murder from the lightning. Self-love preventing the mind from concentration, is identity without form, is no thought as such; law and external influences contained, do not affect. When that giving up all belief, reflects only its meaning, then is there purity of vision, innocence of touch, ergo, self-love. Verily, verily men are born, suffer and die through their belief. Ejaculation is death. Self-<u>love is preservat</u>ion and life.

16. *i.e. his rainbow.*

17. *Chapter on self-attraction omitted.*

18. *This is the test. The one who doubt would naturally submit himself.*

Man to invoke pleasure in his choice, sub-
tracts from desire, his desire is partial desire,
becomes sub-duple (conflict), never is his energy
full. Having no true focus, he is deceived in his
strength and attains a pure measure of pleasure
from his body. In success how heavy is his sen-
tence! Pleasure becomes the illusion. Through
dire necessity, "his means," he is bound to its
cause and effect, and becomes a holcaust on the
pyre of sentiment. This self-love is the only full
energy, all else a wrapping of dissatisfaction, the
hypothesis of desires which obscures.

Man in the misery of his illusions and un-
satisfied desires, wings his flight to different re-
ligions, and doctrines, seeks redeception, a hyp-
notic, a palliative from which he suffers fresh
miseries in exhaustion. The terms of the cure
are new illusions, greater entanglement, more
stagnant environment.

Having studied all ways and means to plea-
sure and pondered over them well again and
again, this self-love has been found by me to be
the only free, true and full one, nothing more
sane, pure, and complete. There is no deceit:
when by this all experience certainly is known,
everything sublimely beautiful and exceedingly
amiable: where is the necessity of other means?

Like the drink to the drunkard everything should be sacrificed for it. This Self-love is now declared by me the means of evolving millions of ideas for pleasure without love, or its synonyms-self-reproach, sickness, old-age, and death. The Symposium of self and love. O! Wise Man, Please Thyself.

THE COMPLETE RITUAL & DOCTRINE OF MAGIC

Ecstasy in Self-love the Obsession

My dearest, I will now explain the only safe and true formula, the destroyer of the darkness of the World, the most secret among all secrets. Let it be secret to him who would attain. Let it cover any period of time, depending on his conception. There is no qualification[19], nor ritual or ceremony. His very existence symbolising all that is necessary to perfection. Most emphatically, there is no need of repetition or feeble imitation. You are alive!

Magic, the reduction of properties to sim-

19. *The means being simplicity, he is comparatively free to make his own qualifications and difficulties, i.e., many retirements are absurd and at once prove his incapacity, the non existence of what he sets about to prove. He at once sets his limit and servility.*

plicity, making them transmutable to utilise them afresh by direction, without capitalization, bearing fruit many times. Know deliberation, over consciousness and concentration to be its resistance and sycophancy, the ultimate acquirement of idiotcy. Whether for his own pleasure or power, the fulfilment of desire is his purpose, he would terminate this by magic. Let him wait for a desire analogous in intensity[20], he then sacrifices this desire (or its fulfilment) to the initial desire, by this it becomes organic, the quantum. He has not attained freedom from law[21]. Hence let him wait for a belief to be subtracted, that period when disillusionment has taken place[22]. Verily disappointment is his chance. "This free entity of belief" and his desire are united to his purpose by the use of Sigils or sacred letters. By projecting the consciousness into one part, sensation not being manifold, becomes intensified. By the abstention of desire, except in the object, this is attained (at the psychological time this

20. *Just a natural desire*

21. *This is a short formula for those whose belief is full in the law, are house holders following their desires. The formula holds good for any purpose.*

22. *Illustration, the loss of faith in a friend, or a union that did not fulfill expectations.*

[74]

determines itself).

By non-resistance (involuntary thought and action), worry and apprehension of non-fulfilment, being transient, find no permanent abode: he desires everything. Anxiety defeats the purpose, it retains and exposes the desire. Conscious desire is non-attractive. The mind quiet and focussed, undisturbed by external images does not distort the sense impressions (there is no hallucination; it would end in imaginative fulfilment), but magnifies the existing desire, and joins it to the object in secret.

Casting the Shadow

The Ego not being totally oblivious, let him retain only and visualise the Sigil form, it is his chalice, the means of vacuity and incarnation. By the deliberation of an analogous emotion at that time, he deputises the law (reaction). Miraculous is he, balance not known in this world imitated (attained). All other consciousness annulled with safety, the vehicle strong enough for the ecstasy, he is beyond hurt. Now let him imagine a union takes place between himself (the mystic union of the Ego and Absolute). The nectar emitted, let him drink slowly, again and again[23]. After this astonishing experience his passion is incomparable, there is nothing in the world he will desire: unless he wills. That is why people do not understand me. The ecstasy in its emotion is omnigenous. Know it as the nectar of life, the Syllubub of Sun and Moon. Verily he steals the fire from Heaven: the greatest act of bravery in the world. Deliberation egotized, except in the refraction[24] of the ecstasy, is exposure and death, becoming a presiding obsession, control having been given to a prior experience and is over-conscious of that through it momentarily finding freedom from its native law; thus generating double personality (Insanity).

By these means there is no desire beyond fulfilment, no accomplishment too wonderful, depending on the amount of free belief[25].

Men of small pleasure and enterprise, obliv-

---

23. *If it becomes physical, let him imagine another's body, he has that sigil or its emergency. This, although not his original purpose, he will and exceedingly amiable.*

24. *Laughter in this case.*

25. *It may be done by localizing desire to one sense, hence by this formula using the ear as the vehicle, one hears the most transcendental music ever conceived, being the voices and harmony of every conceivable animal and human existence and so with each sense.*

ious of your purpose, fault-finding, avaricious, sinful, who cannot live without women or enjoy without pain, fearsome, inconstant, diseased, and withered, dependent, cruel, deceived, and liars, the worst of men! Know, Oh, Lord, Oh beloved Self, I have now told you of that most secret tavern where passion goes when youth has gone, where any man may drink of the nectar of all-beneficent and gratuitous ecstasy. The most pleasurable nourishment that harms no one.

NOTE ON THE DIFFERENCE OF MAGICAL OBSESSION (GENIUS) & INSANITY

MAGICAL obsession is that state when the mind is illuminated by sub-conscious activity evoked voluntarily by formula at our own time, etc., for inspiration. It is the condition of Genius.

Other obsession is the "blind leading the blind," caused by quietism, known as mediumism, an opening out of the Ego to (what is called) any external influence, elementals, or disembodied energy. A transmutated consciousness that is a resistance to "true" sub-conscious activity, it being a voluntary insanity, a somnambulation of the Ego with "no form" or control to guide it: hence its emanations are stupid in suggestion, or memories of childhood.

Obsession known as or related to insanity is an experience that is dissociated from the personality (Ego) through some sort of rejection. It is sub-crystalline, and cannot become permanently attached to the sub-consciousness, not having exhausted or completed itself by realisation. Depending on its degree of intensity and resistance shown at some time or another, the Ego has or has not knowledge of the obsession; always is its expression autonomous, divorced from personal control, power of direction and timing. Concentration determines dissociation. Enthusiasm for one object seeking completion by identification, sacrifices all else, or deliberately forgets. Its separation from the Ego (it becoming equal, or more in bulk than the rest of the consciousness, causes subdivision or "double personality"), is caused by its own intensity or by shock of resistance determined by some incompatibility of the desired or desire.

Concentration is dissatisfied desire, a conflict that can never be satisfied, because of its means. When the Ego, not appearing to have or not knowing the means of fulfilment, seeks its repudiation, repression, imaginative fulfilment, or transmutation to escape its worry. None of these is the desire's or obsession's annihilation, but its separation or concealment from the rest of the Ego, its premature sub-conscious existence. It is held there only when some form of resistance is active, when resistance is dormant-control is given to the presiding obsession, allowing its incarnation in, and swamping of the Ego, which has to live and perform its emotional experience. Disease and Insanity (all disease is insanity) is caused when the disembodied energy has no vital function. It is this energy which is utilised for the vitalization of Sigils.

SIGILS

The Psychology of Believing

If the "supreme belief" remains unknown, believing is fruitless. If "the truth" has not yet been ascertained, the study of knowledge is unproductive. Even if "they" were known their study is useless. We are not the object by the perception, but by becoming it. Closing the gateways of sense is no help. Verily I will make common-sense the foundation of my teaching.

Otherwise, how can I convey my meaning to the deaf, vision to the blind, and my emotion to the dead? In a labyrinth of metaphor and words, intuition is lost, therefore without their effort must be learned the truth about one's self from him who alone knows the truth . . . . yourself.

Of what use the wisdom of Virginity to him who has been raped by the seducer, ignorance? Of what use sciences or any knowledge except as medicine? Hidden treasure does not come at the word nor by digging with your hands in the main road. Even with the proper implements and accurate knowledge of place, etc., may be but the acquisition of what you possessed long ago. There is a great doubt as to whether it is hidden, except by the strata of your experience and atmospheres of your belief.

The pertinent question now proposed by "Thee" should be asked by those desirous of some measure of genius. My answer like the mighty germ is in agreement with the universe, simple and full of deep import and for a time extremely objectionable to your ideas of good and beauty. Listen, attentively, O! Aspirant, all agog for information, to my answer, for by living the meaning thou shalt truly be freed from the bondage of constitutional ignorance. Thou must live it thyself; I cannot live it for thee.

The chief cause of genius is realization or "I" by an emotion that allows the lightning assimilation of what is perceived. This emotion is immoral in that it allows free association of knowledge without the accessories of belief. Its condition is, therefore, ignorance of "I am" and "I am not" with absent-mindedness as believing. Its most excellent state is the "Neither-Neither," the free or atmospheric "I."

You remember in your youth the thought "that this world is a curious place" in the emotion when you felt "why" as to whether this life is a reasonable development? What was the cause of this and of your summarily dismissing it from your mind? Again the feeling that the most commonplace object is magnificently strange and the vague emotion of co-relation between the incompatible (exhaustive arguments often see this, but always excuse it); the curiosity and shock with a more intimate association with the wonders of creation. What is it that prevents you following investigation into "what exactly is surprise," etc.? What is the cause of your believing more in God than a dog-fight? Yet you fear dogs more than God! Where is the difference between yourself choked with disquieting piety, and the innocence of a babe? Perhaps in these is the cause of ignorance.

Belief is the fall from the Absolute. What are you going to believe? Truth seeks its own negation. Different aspects are not the truth, nor are they necessary to truth. Of its emanations which are you to strangle at birth? Are you illegitimate? You believe in right and wrong- what punishment will you determine? Can you escape the driving "Must"? Who can escape boredom- without change? Who remain single and content! What man among you is large and free enough to encompass his "self"? Your belief obfuscates lineage. Ambition is smallness- your customed environment. Remember, time is an unstudied imagination of the experienced. What may be called the early experience was its completion, so of learning there is no finis. What you learn to-morrow is determined by what you have done- the accomplished lesson of yesterday. Never learning to-day what you can do to-morrow is called loss, but is theft from time, wholesomeness and rejuvenescence. Repeat this delay again and again till you arrive at spontaneity, chance in safety. The pursuit of learning (believing) is the grotesque incubator of stupidity.

If you could truly believe, we should realise the virtue of it. We are not free to believe . . . . however much we so desire, having conflicting ideas to first exhaust. Sigils are the art of believing; my invention for making belief organic, ergo, true belief.

When by the wish to believe- it is of the necessity incompatible with an existing belief and is not realized through the inhibition of the organic belief- the negation of the wish, faith moves no mountains, not till it has removed itself. Supposing I wish to be great (is not counting that I am), to have "faith" and believe that I am, does not make me great- even were I to keep up the pretence to the end . . . . it being ceremonial insincerity, the affirmation of my incapacity. I am incapable, because that is the true belief, and organic. To believe differently is but affectation. Therefore the imagination or "faith" that I am great, is a superficial belief. The reaction and denial, caused by the troublesome effervescence of the organic incapacity. Denial or faith does not change or annihilate it, but is its reinforcement and preservation. Therefore belief, to be true, must be organic and sub-conscious. The desire to be great can only become organic at a time of vacuity, and by giving it (Sigil) form.

Spare   [83]

When conscious of the Sigil form (any time but the Magical) it should be repressed, a deliberate striving to forget it, by this it is active and dominates at the unconscious period, its form nourishes and allows it to become attached to the sub-consciousness and become organic, that accomplished, is its reality and realization. He becomes his concept of greatness.

So belief becomes true and vital by striving against it in consciousness and by giving it form. Not by the striving of faith. Belief exhausts itself by confession and non-resistance, i.e., consciousness. Believe not to believe, and in degree you will obtain its existence. Timeliness depending on your morality, give to the poor. If the ambitious only knew it is as difficult to become incapable as it is to become great. They are mutual as accomplishments and equally satisfying.

THE SUB-CONSCIOUSNESS

ALL geniuses have active sub-consciousness, and the less they are aware of the fact, the greater their accomplishments. The sub-consciousness is exploited by desire reaching it. So consciousness should not contain the "great" desire once the Ego has wished: and should be filled with an affected ambition for something different, not vice-versa, the inevitable penalty of cowardice lurking somewhere: surely not an inglorious deceit? Genius, like heroism, is a matter of bravery- you have to forget fear, or incapacity somehow . . . . hence its expression is always spontaneous. How simple it is to acquire genius- you know the means; who will take the plunge? The learning of "How" is the eternal "Why"- unanswered! A genius is such, because he does not know how or why.

The Storehouse of Memories with an Ever-Open Door

Know the sub-consciousness to be an epitome of all experience and wisdom, past incarnations as men, animals, birds, vegetable life, etc., etc., everything that exists, has and ever will exist. Each being a stratum in the order of evolution. Naturally then, the lower we probe into these strata, the earlier will be the forms of life we arrive at; the last is the Almighty Simplicity. And if we succeed in awakening them, we shall gain their properties, and our accomplishment will correspond. They being experiences long passed, must be evoked by extremely vague suggestion, which can only operate when the mind is unusually quiet or simple. To have their wisdom does not mean the necessity of their bodies- the body modifies in relation to "means" (we travel faster than the hunting leopard, but do not have its body), when it is the means it changes accordingly. Now, if we observe Nature, the early forms of life are wonderful in their properties, adaptability, etc; their strength enormous, and some are indestructible. No matter what the desire is, it always is its accomplishment. A microbe has the power to destroy the world (and certainly would if it took an interest in us). If you were to dismember its limb, the mutilated part would regrow, etc. So by evoking and becoming obsessed or illuminated by these existences, we gain their magical properties, or the knowledge of their attainment. This is what already happens (everything happens at all times) though exceedingly slowly; in striving for knowledge we repel it, the mind works best on a simple diet.

The Key to Prophecy

The law of Evolution is retrogression of function governing progression of attainment, i.e., the more wonderful our attainments, the lower in the scale of life that governs them.

Our knowledge of flight is determined by that desire causing the activity of our bird etc. Karmas. Directly our desire reaches the stratum belonginging to those existences that can "fly" without wings- so shall we fly without machines. This sub-conscious activity is the "capacity," the "knowledge"; all other we acquire is of a negative or manurial value. The virtue of learning and acquiring knowledge by the ordinary means is in its worry and disappointment, of that degree which causes exhaustion: by that the desire might accidentally reach the real abode of knowledge, i.e., the sub-consciousness. Inspiration is always at a void moment, and most great discoveries accidental, usually brought about by exhaustion of the mind. My formula and Sigils for sub-conscious activity are the means of inspiration, capacity or genius, and the means of accelerating evolution. An economy of energy and method of learning by enjoyment. A bat first grew wings and of the proper kind, by its desire being organic enough to reach the sub-consciousness. If its desire to fly had been conscious, it would have had to wait till it could have done so by the same means as ourselves, i.e., by machinery. All genius has an hypothesis (usually natural) in the form of a hobby, which serves to restrain and occupy the conscious mind, to prevent its interference with spontaneous expression. The great Leonardo's mathematics, etc., served to "Deceive" him as such an hypothesis (and as Sigils). Our lives are full of the Symbolism of those predominating Karmas we are governed by. All ornament, useless dress, etc., are such (they please people because they feel the identification), and the means of locating them (Karmas). The symbolism of crowning a man King, is that he, resembling God (on earth), has reached the lowest strata of his sub-consciousness (those one-cell organisms if you like), which predominate as governing his functions. (Of course, those crowned Kings are never such, they symbolise the "hope," not the reality.) Hence the floral nature of and precious stones in design of the crown relate to first principles. He is King who has reached the dual principle in its simplicity, the first experience which is all experience . . . . he has no need of crowns and kingdoms.

By Sigils and the acquirement of vacuity, any past incarnation, experience, etc., can be summoned to consciousness. It may even happen in sleep in the form of dreams, but this means is very difficult. [Chapters on day and night dreaming for pleasure omitted.]

Total vacuity is difficult and unsafe for those governed by morality, complexes, i.e., whose belief is not entirely self-love. Hence this desideratum of Sigils, etc.

Know all ritual, ceremony, conditions, as arbitrary (you have yourself to please), a hindrance and confusion; their origin was for amusement, later for the purpose of deceiving other from knowing the truth and inducing ignorance; and as always happens their high priests were the more deceived themselves. He who deceives another deceives himself much more. Therefore know the Charlatans by their love of rich robes, ceremony, ritual, magical retirements, absurd conditions, and other stupidity, too numerous to relate. Their entire doctrine a boastful display, a cowardice hungering for notoriety; their standard everything unnecessary, their certain failure assured. Hence it is that those with some natural ability quickly lose it by their teaching. They can only dogmatise, implant and multiply that which is entirely superficial. Were I a teacher I should not act as master, as knowing more, the pupil could lay no claim to discipleship. Assimilating slowly, he would not be conscious of his learning, he would not repeat the vital mistake; without fear he would accomplish with ease.

The only teaching possible is to show a man how to learn from his own wisdom, and to utilise his ignorance and mistakes. Not by obscuring his vision and intention by righteousness.

SIGILS.
BELIEF WITH PROTECTION

Magickal Obsession.

I will now explain their creation and use; there is no difficulty about it, how pure and clear it all is[26]. Out of love for my foolish devotees I invented it. All desire, whether for Pleasure, Knowledge, or Power, that cannot find "Natural" expression, can by Sigils and their formula find fulfilment from the sub-consciousness. Sigils are the means of guiding and uniting the

---

26. *By this system, you know exactly what (you believe) your Sigil must relate to. If you used any form stupidly, you might possibly "conjure up" exactly what you did not want-the mother of insanity, or what always happens then, nothing at all. This being the only system, any result other than by it is accidental. Also you do not have to dress up as a traditional magician, wizard or priest, build expensive temples, obtain virgin parchment, black goat's blood, etc., etc., in fact no theatricals or humbug.*

partially free belief[27] with an organic desire, its carriage and retention till its purpose served in the sub-conscious self, and its means of reincarnation in the Ego. All thought can be expressed by form in true relation. Sigils are monograms of thought, for the government of energy (all heraldry, crests, monograms, are Sigils and the Karmas they govern), relating to Karma; a mathematical means of symbolising desire and giving it form that has the virtue of preventing any thought and association on that particular desire (at the magical time), escaping the detection of the Ego, so that it does not restrain or attach such desire to its own transitory images, memories and worries, but allows it free passage to the sub-consciousness.

Sigils are made by combining the letters of the alphabet simplified. Illustration, the word "Woman" in Sigil form is

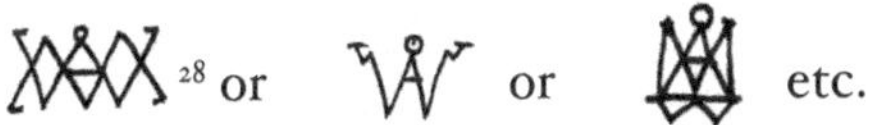

[28] or or etc.

27. *Free belief or energy, i.e., a disappointed desire, not yet an obsession.*

28. *There are six methods of Sigils employed in this book, each corresponding to different strata. The one shown here is illustrative and the fundamental idea of them all, from which anyone can evolve his own system. Conditions, etc., or*

The word tiger 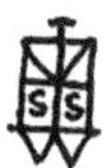 etc., etc. The idea being to obtain a simple form which can be easily visualised at will, and has not too much pictorial relation to the desire. The true method has a much greater virtue, which cannot be explained briefly, being the secret of thought form, as degrees of suggestion, and what exactly is in a name. We have now agreed as to how a Sigil is made, and what virtue it has. Verily, what a person believes by Sigils, is the truth, and is always fulfilled. This system of Sigils is believed by taking it up as a hobby at a time of great disappointment or sorrow. By Sigils I have endowed fools with wisdom, made the wise fools, giving health to the sick and weak, disease to the strong, etc. Now, if for some purpose, you wanted the strength of a tiger- you would make a sentence such as:- "This my wish to obtain the strength of a tiger." Sigilized this would be:-

This my wish

To obtain 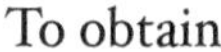 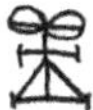

The strength of a Tiger 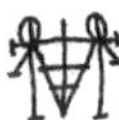

Combined as one Sigil

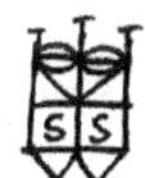 or 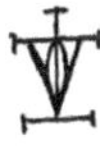

Now by virtue of this Sigil you are able to send your desire into the subconsciousness (which contains all strength); that having happened, it is the desire's realization by the manifestation of the knowledge or power necessary.

First, all consciousness except of the Sigil has to be annulled; do not confuse this with concentration- you simply conceive the Sigil any moment you begin to think. Vacuity[29] is obtained by exhausting the mind and body by some means or

---

29. *This is not the passivity of mediumism which opens the mind to what is called external influence- disembodied energy usually having no better purpose than to rap-tables. There are many means of attaining this state of vacuity: I mention the most simple, there is no need for crucifixion. Drugs are useless. Smoking and laziness the more difficult.*

another. A personal or traditional means serves equally well, depending on temperament; choose the most pleasant; these should be held in favour, Mantras and Posture, Women and Wine, Tennis, and the playing of Patience, or by walking and concentration on the Sigil, etc., etc. None is necessary to him who has (even symbolically) for a moment by the "Neither-Neither" conquered the dual principle (Conception), his Ego is free from gravity. If the Sigil is made an obsession by continual apprehension, its realization may happen at any moment, in the form of inspiration. This is done by reverting the mind to the Sigil when one is extremely worried- the time of exhaustion is the time of fulfilment. At the time of exhaustion or vacuity, retain only and visualize the Sigil form- eventually it becomes vague, then vanishes and success is assured. by the Ego conceiving only the Sigil, and not being able to conceive anything from it, all energy is focussed through it, the desire for identification carries it to the corresponding sub-conscious stratum, its destination. The Sigil being a vehicle, serves the purpose of protecting consciousness from the direct manifestation of the (consciously unacknowledged) obsession, conflict is avoided with any incompatible ideas and neither gains sepa-

[94]

rate personality. It (the obsession) is either gradually assimilated and becomes organic or returns to its original abode, its purpose of illumination served. Hence the mind, by Sigils, depending upon the intensity of desire, is illuminated or obsessed (knowledge or power) from that particular Karma (the sub-conscious stratum, a particular existence and knowledge gained by it) relative to the desire, but not from memory or experience which was recent. Knowledge is obtained by the sensation, resulting from the unity of the desire and Karma. Power, by its "actual" vitalization and resurrection.

This knowledge leaves its stratum in company with the energy or desire returning to the Ego. It escapes the Ego's resistance by associating with similar images, memories, or experiences relative (recieved in this life), that the mind contains, and crystalizes itself by their symbolism. Hence most illumination is symbolic, and must be subsequently translated.

[Chapters on Symbolism, Automatic Drawing As Means To Art, & Note on Sacred Letters omitted.]

ON MYSELF

Conceiving, thou hast given no sign of life. In claiming thee, a labour of creating value, is nothing worth holding, nothing satisfying; the realization of thy inhibition all? By self-effacement would seem reality. This self, how empty! how prolific of incompleteness! In self-denial its stimulation to simulate reality . . . . more and more comes out- these ugly mists of illusion are parental, the cause of Heaven's hatred! That is why I fear to believe in God, subordination to an attribute, an idea of Self is not freedom of love! Probably Almighty is he who is unconscious of the idea of God. Now may the fierceness of my unity be "Thy" silence and for me no longer a query or labour to espouse my doubt. Yet mankind for ever doubts, quirks, and for every pleasure pays, till he becomes millionary: the punishment shall fit the appraisement of his capitalization, there is that fear! The rich in dross, to cheat his conscience, affects humility, speaks of himself as "poor," his possessions as "burdens," or of "small account"! Of what consolation the truth in the day of weary waiting and watching, the restless striving, the imprisonment, the rack, the horrors of every conceivable torture? When he becomes accustomed, loses reality, and no longer deterred, will he then create God and miseries afresh? Oh, folly of the world, deny thy faith, renounce this Bloody-Sceptred God and confess. The completion of folly is the beginning of childhood, but of knowledge there is no end. It was the straying that found the path direct. From childhood, I have never denied my invincible purpose. Oh, silent watcher, thou sleepless eye of the Universe, watch over the beginning of all my ideas. The misery of the world would seem eternal, whilst I, in the midst, like an infant not yet smiling, am impervious in purity (of self-love) but I dare not claim its service! I am in eternal want of realization, poor though I be, my contentment is beyond your understanding. An opinionist, I fear to advocate an argument, or compromise myself by believing my own doctrines as such . . . . may they ever be their own expurgers! Fearsome of knowledge, may my belief be its emptiness, yea, ignorance! From my daring to believe religions, doctrines, creeds, so shall I hold the jewel of truth. So cautious am I, simultaneously do I deny that which I affirm, and hold fast to the "not-necessity," by paradox superseded, without antecedent, spontaneous,

I revert to the Absolute, watch my intoxication and control- the reaction of Karma. How easy is the Way, it would seem as though nothing should be said but all unsaid! May my words be few and pregnant! Alas, the futility of the idea of God has not yet reached its limit, all men liars, appear striving for insanity as its climax: while I alone as one prematurely aged, reason tottering on its throne, remain sane, in positive chastity, confessing no conscience, no morals- a virgin in singleness of purpose.

THE FOCUS OF LIFE

The Mutterings of AAOS

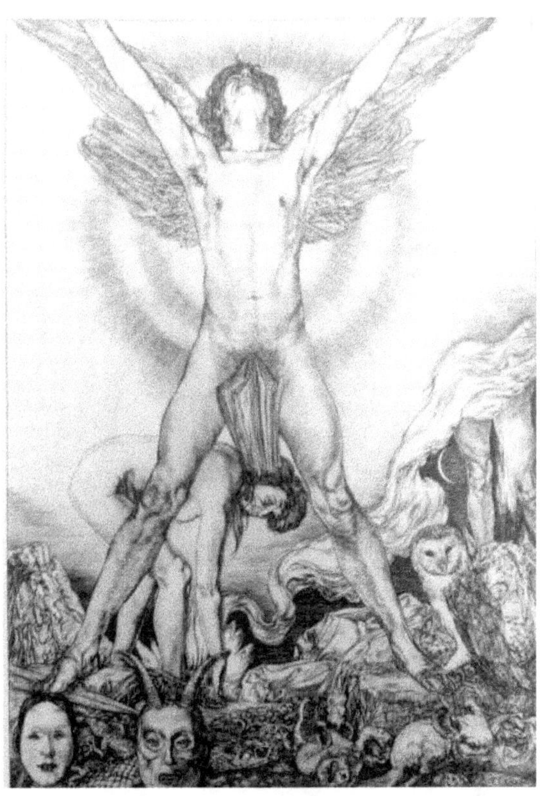

Now For Reality

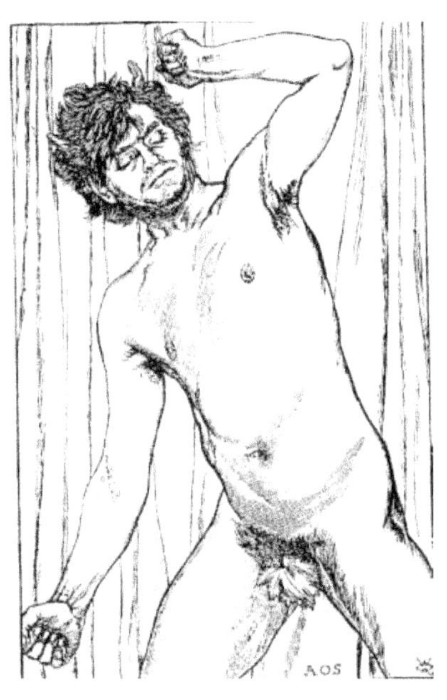

Aaos Recovers from the Death Posture

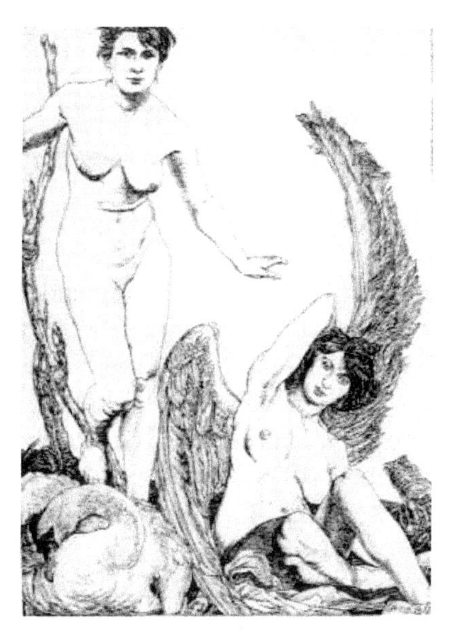

Nature is more atrocious

APHORISM I
"The effort of remembering in the Valley of Fear."

Kia of the Effigies Speaks of Zos in Soliloquy

I bring a sword that contains its own medicine: The sour milk that cureth the body. Prepare to meet God, the omnifarious believing,-Thyself the living truth. Die not to spare, but that the world may perish. Nature is more atrocious. Learning all things from Thee in the most sinister way for representation: from thy thought to become thereafter. Having suffered pleasure and pain, gladly dost thou deny the things of existence for freedom of desire-from this sorry mess of inequality-once so desired. And is fear of desire. The addition of the 'I' of a greater illusion. Desire is the conception I and induces Thou. There is neither thou nor I nor a third person-loosing this consciousness by unity of I and Self; there would be no limit to consciousness in sexuality. Isolation in ecstasy, the final inducement, is enough-But, procreate thou alone! Speak not to serve but to scoff. Hearest thou, heaven's loud guffaw? Directly the mouth opens it speaks righteousness. In the ecstatic laughter of men I hear their volition towards release. How can I speak that for which I have necessitated silence? Salvation shall be Unsay all things: and true, as is time, that speaketh all things. Of what use are hints or stage whispers? True wisdom cannot be expressed by articulate sounds. The language of fools-is words. In the labyrinth of the alphabet the truth is hidden. It is one thing repeated many times. Confined within the limits or rationalism; no guess has yet answered. O Zos, thou art fallen into the involuntary accident of birth and rebirth into the incarnating ideas of women. A partial sexuality entangled in the morass of sensual law. On earth the circle was fabricated. The origin of all things is the complex self. How shall it be made the end of things? Dubious of all things by this increase, and ignorance of individuality. I or Self, in conflict, separate. This forgetfulness of symboli becomes the unexplored 'reason' of existence. Unable to conceive the events of the present: what shall be knowledge of past and future? Verily, this creator speaks 'I know not what I do.' And in this living nightmare, where all is cannibalism. Why dost thou deny thyself? Verily, Man resembles his creator, in that he consumes himself in much filth. Heaven gives indiscriminately of its superabundance to make the ghastly struggle called existence. The necessity was a deliberate serving of its own pleasure-becoming more alien. Remoteness from self is pain and precocious creation. Through this remoteness from Self-thou dost not hear thine own call to be potentially Thyself. The living self does not habitate. There is no truth in thy wish. Pleasure wearies of thee. Ecstatic fulfilment of ecstasy, is it asking too much? Alas, the smallness of man's desire! Thou shalt suffer all things once again: unimagined sensations, and so consume the whole world. O Zos, thou shalt live in millions of forms and every conceivable thing shall happen unto Thee. Remember these senses are that which thou hast desired. What is all thought but a morality of the senses that has become sex? What is desired of the Self is given-eventually. The desire is sufficient. The 'Self,' will pleasure in all things. There is only one sense,-the sexual. There is only one desire,-procreation. I am the cause-thou the effect. I am all that I concieve.

Not for all time but at some time. 'I multiply I' is creation: The sexual infinity. There is no end to the details of my extreme likeness. The more chaotic-the more complete am I. The soul is the ancestral animals. The body their knowledge. This omnivorous soul, how lusty: it would seem to be everlasting in its suicide. These modified sexualities are the index of knowledge; this realized; the dualities do not obstruct with associations that involve infinite complexities and much education. Existence is a continuation of self-realization. To create value where there is none. By all desire being one there is no overlapping nor the later necessity of undesiring. Complex desire is the further creation of different desire, not the realization of [particular] desire. O Zos, Thou shall die of extreme youth! Death is a disease of fear. All is a backward walking-realized incapacity of volition: To walk towards thyself. With thine infinite self multiplication of associations Thou knowest all things. Among sentient creatures human birth is highly desirable, man desires emancipation-liberation to his primeval self. Remember! Didst thou leave the high estate for worse things? Man becomes what he relapses into.

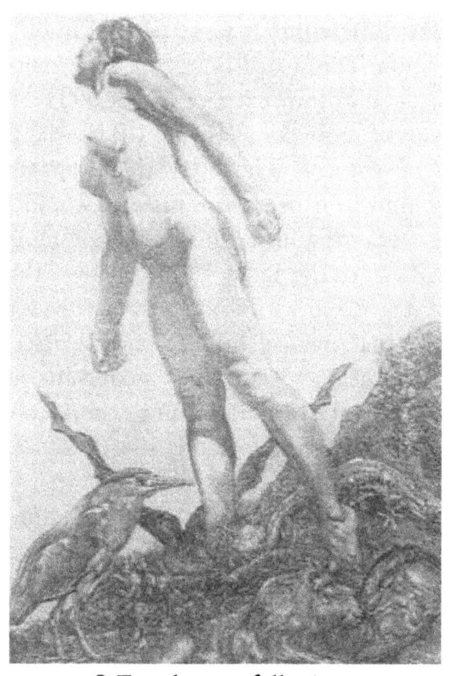

O Zos, thou art fallen into...
the incarnating ideas of women

Cast into demoniacal moulds, human nature is the worst possible nature. The degenerate need women, dispense with that part of thyself. Give unto her all thy weaknesses, it is the suffering half. Pain awaits him, who is sentimentally desirous. Be it thus: 'Woman, there shall be no vintage from our kisses'. In man and woman is thy 'being.' But I say, Thou could'st create this body anew. Awake! The time has come for the new sexualities! Then would be occasion for greater pleasures. To improve the species ye men must love one another. This old illusion of righteousness has gained a future state wherein men labour every doubt. Thou art that which thou dost prefer. The seer, the instrument of seeing, or the seen. Conscious desire is the negation of possession: the procrastination of reality. Make thy desire subconscious; the organic is creative impulse to will. Beware of thy desire. Let it be something that implies nothing but itself. There are no differences-only degrees of sensation. Provoke consciousness in touch, ecstasy in vision. Let thy highest virtue be: "Insatiety of desire, brave self-indulgence and primeval sexualism." Realization is not by the mere utterance of the words 'I am I' nor by self-abuse, but by the living act. If the desire for realization exists in thee, sensouous objects will continually provide conveniences. Realization of this Self, which is all pleasure at will, is by consciousness of one thing in belief. To be the same is the difficulty. Thought is the negation of knowledge. Be thy business with action only. Purge thyself of belief: live like a tree walking! Take no thought of good or evil. Become self-active causality by Unity of thine, I and Self. Reality exists but not in consciousness of such: this phenomenal 'I' is noumenal and neither-neither. Now thus is concentration explained: "The will, the desire, the belief; lived as inseparable, become realization." Truth concerns exactitude of belief, not reality. He who has no law is free. In all things there is no necessity. Become weary of devising wisdom in morals. Many unseemly words have been spoken in self slander, what more painful than that? For in the mud I tread on thee. The path men take from every side is mine. There is nothing more to be said. 'I'-infinite space.

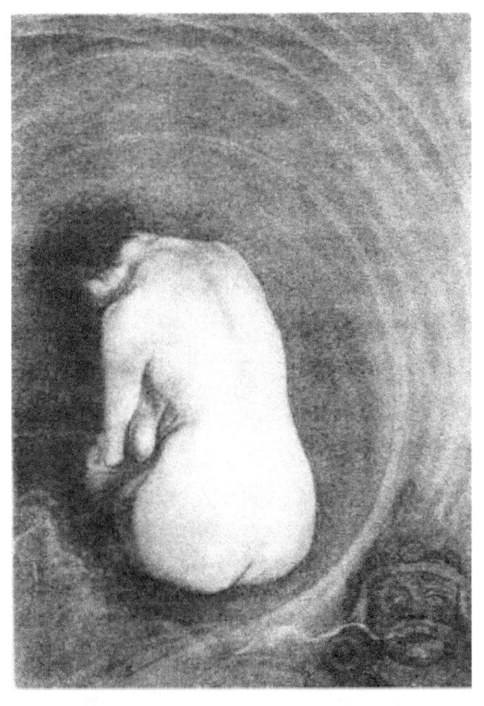

The Soul is the Ancestral Animals

APHORISM II
"Morals of shadow, wherein the Arcana of Zos has no commandments"

Zos Speaks of Ikkah:

Leaving aside all unreal dreams, consider this world as insincere disbelief. Lo this day salvation has come. My 'I and Self' has agreed in belief. I would ask of thee thy suppressed self. Is it not the new thing desired? No man shall follow me. I am not thy preservation. Thou art the way. Assuredly, thy virtue is to be equally different. Thy complaint is the calamity: The hypocrite is always at prayer. Dost thou suffer? Thou shalt again suffer, till thine I does not fear its body. Rather seek and increase by thy temptations, it is but the way to intelligence. Transgression is wiser than prayer: Make this thy obsession. Thank only thyself and be silent. The coward's

way is religion. There is no fear-but righteous-
ness. Let this be thy one excuse, I pleasured my-
self. Brave laughter-not faith. Rewarded are the
courageous for they shall pass! Thine I is envi-
ous of satisfaction. Yet none devotes himself to
reality. Whoever learneth much, unlearneth all
sentimental and small desires. This is the new
atavism I would teach: Demand of God equal-
ity-usurp! The mighty are righteous for their
morals are arbitrary. Live beyond thought in
courageous originality. These hopes and fears
are somnism, there is little reality. Repent not,
but strive to sin in thine own way, light-heart-
edly: without self-reproach. One becomes the
thing itself or its creature. Judge without mercy,
all this weakness is thy self-abuse. Experience is
by contract. The great experience: Seduce thy-
self to pleasure. There is only one sin-suffering.
There is only on virtue-the will to self-pleasure.
The greatest- the greatest non-morally. The ori-
gin of morality is obedience to the earliest form
of government. In youth, all things have to obey
their parents. O, my aged IKKAH, loose this the
navel cord, that my youth may pass! The most
important outcome of human effort is that we
learn to become righteous thieves: To possess
more easily of others for self-advantage. In

this incessant glorification of work, I discover a great human secret: "Do thou the work-I my pleasure." As above so below, this is never sufficiently realized. . . . Remorse? Nay, do unto thyself all things, fearlessly. Finality is reached when ye have learned to digest everything. What is all man-slaughter but what ye have done unto yourself? Only where there is necessity is there death. Dispense with all 'means' to an end. There is nothing higher than joyous sensation. Eternal Self! these millions of bodies I have outworn! Oh, sinister ecstasy. I am thy vicious self pleasure that destroyeth all things. Distrust thy teacher, for 'divine truth' has prevented better men from wisdom. In such revelation there is no suggestion. Do thy utmost unto others: But be surely what thou wilt: and keep thy belief free of morality. Observe thyself by sensation: thus know the finer perturbations and vibrations. This much shalt thou learn: To love all men, for there will be compulsion.

Serve no man, hell is democracy. Think not the words 'I wish,' say not the words 'I will.' Respect thy body: it will again become thy parents. Fear nothing,-strike at the highest. Ennui is fear: Death is failure. Go where thou fearest most. How canst thou become great among men?...

[114]

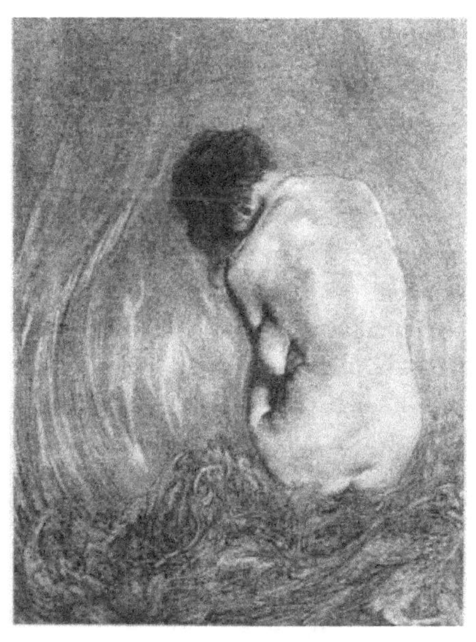

Which are but living their...
peculiarities by a mechanism

Cast thyself forth! Of this event, genius is the successful effort of memory. Break thy commandments, be lawless unto all dogma. Revolt is the fertiliser of the new faculties. Knowledge and all evil wars react from previous existences that are now fragmentary to the body and operate as disembodied astrals. The more distant the creature that govern our functions the more unusual is our manifestation of phenomena, which are but living their physical peculiarities by a mechanism. Retrogress to the point where knowledge ceases, in that law becomes its own spontaneity and is freedom. If my word has spoken unto fragments, pushed aside marriage beds, and brushed out old grave chambers; if I ever rejoiced in calumnies, if I have murdered, lied, adulterated, robbed; if like the weather I spit on all things-is it because I remember, that of my belief-there is a volition that willeth opposite? For I love thee, O Self! For I love thee, O mine I! Oh! how could I fail to be agog for originality in self-love? Never yet has procreation with another been satisfactory. If I have wandered into marriage with anything-there has been a conspiracy of accidents: within and without. And what willeth to self-pleasure- this out-breather of good taste, this conversion to ungodliness? I know thee! . . . thou heavenly necessity that compelleth chance to supersede the sexualities! For mine I is worthy of the Self: and alone knows what is righteousness. Verily, I tell you good and evil are one and the same. It is but the distance thou hast reached. Will unto self-love - the unexhausted, the procreative of ecstasy! Where there is life there is will unto pleasure-however paradoxical the manifestation. Where living things command they risk nothing but their own law. This Self-love does not circumscribe nor promise but gives whatsoever is taken-spontaneously. Thus I teach thee, will unto pleasure of all things, for they must again change the tenacity to obedience. And this new name I give unto thee, for all accusations: Not sinner, but somnambulist. For he who premeditates, acts in his sleep. Having overcome the difficulty of obtaining a male incarnation from parents not too venereal, one's habitation should be wandering among men: Employment, devotion to Art: Bed, a hard surface: Clothes of camel hair: Diet, sour milk and roots of the earth. All morality and love of women should be ignored. To whom does not such abandonment give the unknown pleasure? Again I say: 'In all things' pleasure Thyself, for occasion need not be.

APHORISM III
"The Chaos of the Normal"

Ikkah Speaks of Himself

I would counsel closed ears, for those who contain the great Ideas, have no opinions. Who doth know what his own subconsciousness contains? Still less his own Arcana. They are the great who allow its operation by silence. Of two things we have choice: degeneration or immobility. Out of the past cometh this new thing. Becoming heaven's slaves-is some of pleasure begged again? Man strives for increase,-the monstrous world of vague and mad Ideas is incarnating. Come back, your goal is jail! Turn about and you arrive ..... This maddest of worlds. Daily is pleasure limited by the necessity of cheapened facilities. Onwards and ever more weary-till sleep-then backwards. There is nothing conceivable that does not exist, because the vision is feeble. In keeping the right distance from

Things, is Safety. But how much should we gain? Experience is ignorance. The necessity of reoccurrence. One thing is certain: we are subject to our own moral laws, whether we are or are not aware of them. The desire determines, and no later belief shall alter it one whit. The highest creations are those that harmonize the most incongruous things. Art is the truth we have realized or our belief. The great human factor in Life is deceit: Always the greater deceiver-self? The wrath is revealed against all that hold the truth in righteousness. Still are those shallownesses, who could know they hide a universe? And tell me, what is it the obvious does not contain? Know much of life! Should death give you its secret? Self suggestion-to will, this is the great teacher: not dogma. To those of fixed Ideas, beware of suppressed evacuation. What the world reveres most, treat with the utmost contempt. Consumption, evacuation, sleep: this labour suffers of no variation for to-morrow we again procreate life. O, fool! suicide does not exist . . . there is no death. Death is change and for many very small change. You who stink like a butcher's shambles-what is your daily menu? Become less carnivorous. If the food is wholesome, the body shall not suffer. The difference between man and beast is one of acquisition, not digestion. There is no lasting peace-ye eternally fall in love with the new thing of belief. To the mental gymnast: your somersault returns from the place where it began. Slave! All you know for certain-you suffer. Embrace reality by imagination. From birth is a degeneration of function-safe is he who never leaves his mother's womb. What is perfect does not reflect its caricature. What is true has no argument-in that it is voliton. The workers of malignity own the Kingdom of Earth. What asses these teachers, prophets and moralists now appear! And through them what greater she-asses we have become! You would have prophecy? First tell me your sleeping partner's name . . . . What once evoked a mighty passion-is now repulsive; lest ye forget: sleep alone. If you yourself cannot be ungodly-then nothing will convert you.

No nearer the goal for life is eternal. Which are more unclean: they who make a profession of their morality, or they who prostitute? Life is a vicious charity from which germinates friendships towards parasites. The necessity of a better life is intoxication but more and greater things than strong drink intoxicate. Thou hast become remote-I rejoice in thee! Who invented such things as vanity and humiliation? The higher the

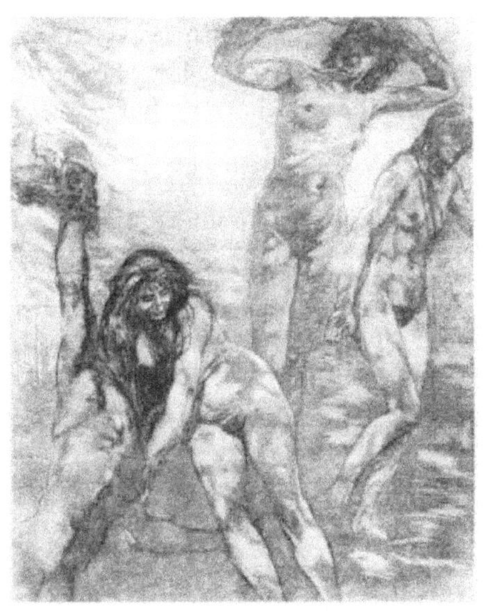

All things are possible even in nightmares

form of creation the more it habitates earth and the more it is conscious of body. Everything that is half realized becomes the material of dreams; man has always badly mixed the dream with the reality. He who transcends time escapes necessity. The living Lord speaks: 'In disciples is my satisfaction.' A weary one asked: 'Is it not written on the sandals of the prostitute-follow me?' All undesirable things become morally fearsome

Only the animal in man dances . . . Hatred is life-the love of possession. He who can truthfully say-I believe in nothing but myself-in all things realized.

Zod-ka Speaks of Ikkah

The abyss Self projecting from non-existence the procreatrix I, was the great change and the beginning: to extend the purpose of desire-for Time to make all existence inexact-those things kept ever vague. Thus was the will to operate unbegotten. One thing is nominally, everything alternatingly desirous. That which is first desired is permitted, then externalized and taken away by a circumlocution of beliefs becoming law. No knowledge would separate us from the virtues of non-existence but that for man-having become involved with disease, all his food is poisonous; his complete saturation is inevitable that he may become again healthy. Thus man wills by thought. By the 'death posture' (A simulation of death by the utter negation of thought, i.e. the prevention of desire from belief and the functioning of all consciousness through the sexuality) [not for subjection of mind, body or longevity nor any thing as such] the Body is allowed to manifest spontaneously and is arbitrary and impervious to reaction. Only he who is unconscious of his actions has courage beyond good and evil: and is pure in this wisdom of sound sleep. Will to pleasure is the basic function underlying all activity whether conscious or not,-and whatsoever the means. Denial of this Self-love is disease-the cause of homicide; the sufferings of part-sexualities and small things germinating. Knowledge of necessities is desirous:-Deliberation is but a sorry disatisfaction-a first cause of illusions, harnessing man to a mass of half-realized desires. Remember! O Ikkah, these present Ideas of consciousness obtaining in senses and bodies, are transitory-are destined for usage and other predeterminations-and unnecessary to wakefulness. Will is transition; the painful process of transmigration-the labour of birth of death. Volition to supersede a thing is inability to realize the living Self. For whatever is attained is but the re-awaking of an earlier experience of body. Man should most desire a simultaneous consciousness of his separate entities. All consciousness of 'I' is a decline and vegetates good and evil afresh-the compulsion of limit and morality. From spontaneous nonexistence, germinate all significant ecstasy-that shall last in the uttermost impossibilities unconditioned to will. Alas! what ornaments are grave-yards? The pleasure ground of self is contact with the living. The fool hastens to man with a mouth overfull of new discoveries of power subservient to will! What matters it that we have realized a little more of I? Of beyond its limits of possibility?

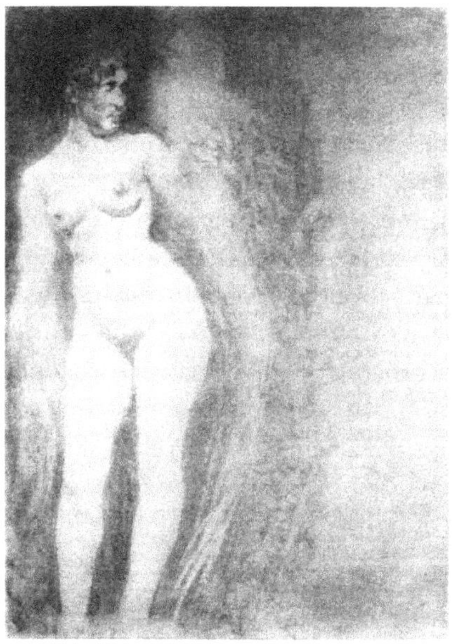

Abandon this haunted mortuary in a blind turning

Note well! All things are possible even in nightmares-becoming, they are a necessity, an additional boundary to memory-the further separate entities of consciousness. Remember O Ikkah! Thou shall not cease to be again what is denied-unto the end of conception: thus man has constructed his seed. These sentient creatures and the beyond conceptions in the order of evolution were thou once as they? O Ikkah, Thou art this present God-this termite and many other things not yet domesticated or associated with thought. This focus 'I' called consciousness is unaware of its entire living embodiments but alternates and epitomizes their personalities. What is 'I' and the extent of its conscious habitation?. . . A weak desire, a memory governed by ethics and ignorant of its own bodies. Therefore that which is indeliberate is the more vital and is will: discarded knowledge is the sexuality and becomes law. Thus entity exists in many units simultaneously without consciousness of 'Ego' as one flesh. Verily, I say-the deliberations of many exist in living animations-their consciousness split among a multitude of creatures but knowing only the more important [?] incarnations-What greater misery than this? Of others, their awake-consciousness is aware of more than one entity and obtain ecstasy by saturable desire. O Ikkah! Jest viciously! Abandon this haunted mortuary in a blind turning-by significant courage. The 'I' surfeit-swelled is the end of compassion-the indrawing of sex to Self-love. Fortunate is he who absorbs his female bodies-ever projecting-for he acquires the extent of his body. Whatever is desired, predetermines its existence in endless ramifications miserably and evanescent: Self-love is the paradox of I. Oh Ikkah Zod-ka! Thy fiction of finality has prevented sleep and created eternity. O, invent sound sleep by the utter ruin of cosmos! For impalpably and anterior to consciousness-all things exist.... With sensibility and name, becoming its living simulation and thus it disappears-involving its consequent necessity. Reason has become too sensible, thus desire has become legerdemain mixed with diablerie. The soul, proud and blighted . . . is a civil war of desire: thereof the necessity for medicine and anesthesia. Man has made this environment: the mind is now the belly of the sexuality. Thus I suggest to thee- Self-love and its own temptation to excess. Verily, greater courage hath none than to satisfy the unexpected desire by Self-pleasure. For this reason, that when the desire again reacts, to op-

erate in the ego, the suffering shall be ecstatic.
How do I know? Not by farcical dialogue with
Self but through contact with its undulations...
are we not ever standing on our own volcano?
What is beyond man-something more dishonest
or a further beast? One thing is desired, another
is thought; and a different becomes. Everything
loved obtains an obscene disease. These dream
postures are ominous prophecy of thyself to be-
come-the obscure wish. O joy and woe! which
is the higher morality-to love man while being
man or to reincarnate as woman to fulfil desire?
Death is that degeneration, an alternation of ego
in consciousness [i.e., desire], its metamorphosis
into separate entities for that purpose: serving
its own. Man's living virtues are those unfamiliar
with names. His absurd I is ever supralapsarian.
Man has exhausted his courage by imaginations
engendered from the damned: Never can he sat-
isfy what follows these repressions. Thou who
tremblest all over! Thy soul shudders! Thou dost
perish from the poison of yesterday's armour
and righteousness! O incomprehensible synon-
ymy! O thou who art neither the vigorous kiss
of my twin sexes nor its writhings of hatred and
black shame. Nothing is discovered of thee un-
til I invented it: from the ceaseless resurrection

of earlier deliberations. O thou syzygy of my I and Self! Thou becomest volatile to whatsoever is sensed. Art thou the hidden wish for madness and hysteric love? O thou "untamed" within, thou shall not lose virtue-for thee I will not domesticate while generating. O idiocy! where is that path where I may wander naked in frenzy, a trespasser against all things reasonable? O time! saith good and evil: 'Come, come! Ego, I come!'

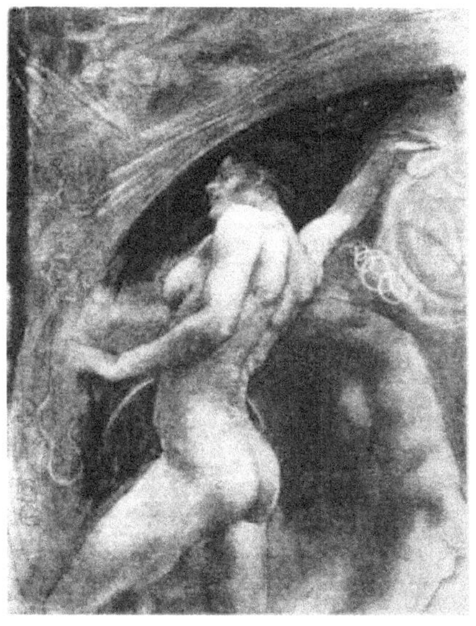

Laughing Aloud, Zos Answered

....Knowledge alone is transitory, the illusion subsequent to 'I desire all things.' Eternal, without beginning is Self; without end am I; there is no other power and substance. The ever changing modifications and diversities we see are the results of forgetfulness, misinterpretated by nightmare senses. When the Self again desires, then I only and nothing else shall remain. Permitting all things, whatsoever is imagined comes out of it. Believe what you will, it has no compassion. The connotation Self-love is applicable to all things. To it, all things are equal. The destroyer of devotees; lover of all things unique. Giving overflow to all who are indifferent to wanglers, who jest at doctrines . . . of emancipation in celibacy and vituperation. I declare this Self-pleasure alone is free of Theism; the disenthralment of God and the distractions of ego in the many entities of existence I show. Ye who praise Truth thereby causing its necessity are compelled to live differently. Out of this afterthought of belief-thrives this somnambulating generation of unpleasured fools, liars and homicides-ever bewildered by good and evil. All has become inborn sex, so complex 'am I,' that a successful awakening is impossible without catastrophe. Birth is now painful, life a dire necessity and death an uncertainty-except of fearsome things. What further, O Ikkah, should a cesspool of truths contain? Nor truth, nor women, nor anything else once made objective shall satisfy. They who are committed to doctrines shall continue to move in this cycle of transmigrating belief: degenerating beyond limits they dare not face, and so allow conception to exist of itself from the imaginations 'I believe.' What more disgusting? For I am all sex. What I am not is moral thought, simulating and separating. Imagined through forgetfulness, born asleep, whose very essence is vague, how can this world with such vapid antecedents, be anything but unthinkable! What man prohibits and then commits will certainly cause suffering, because he has willed double. Born of complex desire, results of actions are dual: multitudinous virtue and vice. Creation is causee through this formula of reaction and is a servile believing-all this universe has come out of it. When by that unprohibiting Self-love all this cosmos is certainly familiar and pleasured, it should be practised with labour. But who is honest enough to believe this without relapse? Having renounced both good and evil conveniently, one should engage in spasmodic madness. Renouncing everything else take shelter in that Self-love, which incites the functions into the bold, 'freedom from necessity am I': virtue and vice shall cease. Self-illumination am I; the procreatrix of this universe. Indomitable in body: born of the bastard truth I made. When the eyes are shut the world certainly does not exist. O chaos! is there no greater joy than flagellation; the ecstatic paralysis that makes holocausts of withered souls; the hideously pitiable cripples-"I fear . . . "? I assert this Self-love to be a most secret ritual hidden by blasphemous Ideographs: and he who calls, pronouncing the word fearlessly, the entire creation of women shall rush into him.

What are lies-but mistimed events?

What is time but a variety of one thing?

What is all folly, but will?

What are all beliefs but the possibilities of I?

What is all future but resurrection?

What is all creation but thyself?

Why is all existence? Awake! Up! up, for thine

    own sake-

Self-love discover.

Spare [131]

O sin, where is thy violence?

O love, where is thine incest?

O thought, where is thy courage?

O hope, where is thy faith?

O Self where is thy humility?

O truth, where is thy mispronunciation?

Verily, Self-love alone is complete!

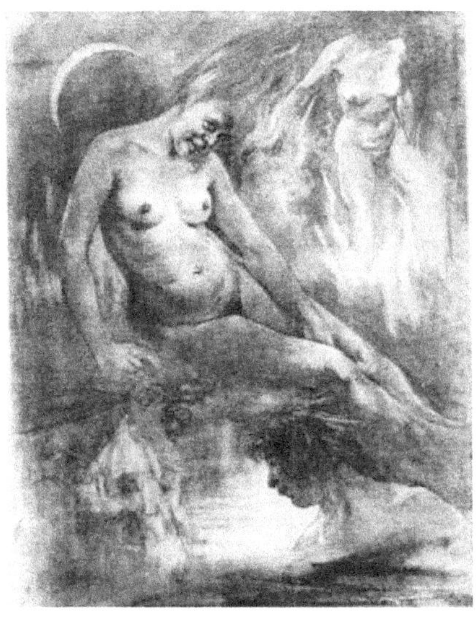

Something Resurrected from an Archetype

The Sexuality and Sleep of Aaos

Aaos having realized at an early age that all systems of belief, religion and rituals; consisted alone in their original value to their creators; And were of the weary, to incarnate pleasure by hope, control by fear; and to Deify by morals; That cowards fear, and must needs promise pleasure of their sufferings; And they who had experienced "I," would have you destroy its body; and potential: Verily, Aaos realized that the origin of I, was for pleasurable procreation... but that things had been changed. Aaos then pondered in his heart long over the geometry of the world of senses; and spake thus: "How far short has realization fallen from original conception? Have we not lived all things previous to the event? What is any desire but all desire? But men get married and nothing is sufficiently arbitrary. I am the origin of all creation, certain it is that I want not salvation, [observing all the miserably diseased mob:] "O, grant that I may add to the world a far greater suffering!" God is a precocious creation of the Apes, something that must be suppressed: Man must regain his sexuality. What is man-this feeder on dead bodies of Self? . . . A mole, a carnivorous plant, a disease of himself, a conglomeration of-

"it was" and a cause, effecting the miscarriage of his desires-ever creating his future necessities: What man knoweth the perturbations of his own fear? Verily, suffering is its own reward. He who willed, knoweth not his own offspring. Man projects a vague 'Self' and calls it truth and many other qualified names: Verily, once a Thing is named it becomes nothingness to its meaning. All happiness is an illusion and a sorry snare. All righteousness is a dishonesty and all sin a pleasure. Assuredly, the courageous alone seem safe ...without remorse. Man invented Self-pleasure but knoweth not his own love. Everything was once arbitrary. Yet they who spoke: their power has ended in common sexual practice-abnormal only with jaded appetites. They who knew were rightly crucified, scorned, ignored and their mouths sealed with their own excrement. Have we not forgotten more than we shall ever learn? Where is the magic to revitalize the mouldering words? Everything is again eventually arbitrary! What is there to believe that is free of belief? What is there to will that is safe from reaction? Why is belief always incarnating? Though oft times not even a sincere wish? Who among men knoweth what he believes? Everything is true at some time. What is this unpleasant Thing, necessity-suffering? How originated pain? What is necessity-but conditioned belief? What is it we eternally desire and say, through disease? Verily, directly a man speaketh-he suffers. What is Self and I? And all these myriad forms called creation-all so essentially like me? Who can realize this Self-portraiture of all Things? Verily, the sexuality has no limit in conception. Whither I would go, there had I long been before. Eternal re-occurence would seem necessary to greater multiplicity! For what reason this loss of memory by these bewilding refractions of my original image,-that I once made-and out of which spring the sexes? God is born again of desire, call it by whatever name: this unmanifested memory has no name till belief incarnates. Hence it may be called,-the re-occuring sub-division of 'I'. Everything becomes necessary. Man is subject to his own law: All else is an obscene jest and a lie. Thus reasoned Aaos in his youth and went to sleep alone. After a vilely repulsive nightmare Aaos awoke saying: "Quiescent are my depths, who could realize They contain such criminal abortions of the cosmos?" What is all body but materialized desire? What are dreams but unsatisfied desires striving to foretell their possibility in despite of morals? Life is but will, that has become organic after satiety; its further desires striving for Unity. Death is that further will incarnating in body. The next day Aaos spoke unto his growing beard: "Destroy O, my Self, these hallucinations of I am not by knowledge of pleasure." Thou mighty ecstasy that willeth Thy pleasure in suffering! Make my consciousness reality of thee in body! What is Self but Cosmos? What is I but Chaos? Eternally creating its pleasure, everything could become arbitrary. Whatever deceit we practice, the functions of the emotions are one; their expression dual: Time making multitudinous by denial. What is experience, but denial? What is the centre, but belief? After a long suspiration, Aaos spoke aloud to his 'I': "Awake, my Self-love! Leave this hour of cow-dust, I am all things to pleasure. Too long have I lived the nightmares of others in my sleep . . . Arise! get forth and feed from the mighty udder of Life. Thou art not a cowherd, nor grass, neither cows no kine! But once again, a creator of cows-who loves their breasts! Are not all things cows to thy pleasure-whether they would or not? And what is Cow? Is it not a fountain? Didst thou not create God, teach nature all secrets and crowd the spaces with cows of desire, unknown and manifesting? Didst thou not create and destroy Woman?"

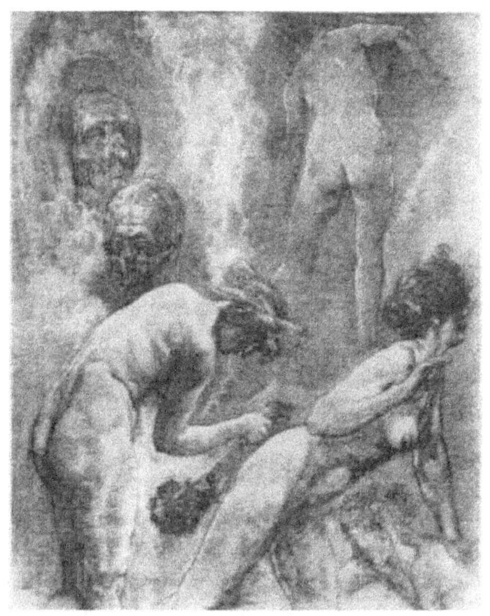

Once Again to Earth

Again Aaos spoke, but unto his lidless eye: "Behold thou hoary, white headed, thou silent watcher of night and day: thou death-clutch on the smallnesses of Time! This neither-neither I, shall transvalue ennui, fear, and all diseases to my wish. Dead is my misery in suffering! How could it exist in my Zodiac, unwilled? I, who transcend ecstasy by ecstasy meditating Need not be in

Self-love! Verily, this constant ecstasy I indraw from Self-creation. By castrating 'of,' my belief is balanced: my arbitrary automatism serving its diverse self-pleasure." Then Aaos meditated and murmured: "All things exist by me: all men exist in me, yet who doth not turn away from his own superabundance while realizing? All desire is for unity: thus my vision seeth through mine ears. Let my unity be realized sufficiently, thus shall my sexuality be convenient unto itself and escape the conceivable . . . Where is lust when the tests wither? Verily these senses have a further purpose beyond their own: thus shall thou steal the fire from Heaven. All things return to their earliest functions." At that moment Aaos realized he was not alone; and a voice asked: "Hast thou no fear?" Laughing aloud, Aaos answered: "Hidden from thy small susceptibilities, monstrous enormities are committed! On the day my wind bloweth a little the cow-dust away-thou O fool, shalt vomit hot blood at thine own prostitution and incest. When thou knowest not, the lust wills non-rationally, the belief bindeth with modest Ideas; the body is subject and suffers. What man can prevent his belief from incarnating? Who is free of filth and disease? All men are servile to the great unconsciousness of their purpose in desire. The I thinks, the Self doth. There is no salvation from desire, neither day nor night does it cease its lengthy procreation of cause and effect: penetrating all things inexplicably. Endless are its elements and nothing whatsoever escapes its embrace-but its own Self-love...Should I fear my I?" Aaos lowering his voice, uttered: "What further use shall I give my sexuality? Verily it is alway speaking for me! This I, non-resisting to the Self, becomes irresistible." When the voice had left Aaos went his way muttering and smiling: "Can it be possible that dead wives resurrect?" For he thought that-Woman was dead. With this reflection Aaoss became silent. Awaking from his Self-introspection he spake aloud to his body: "Man is something that has resurrected from an archetype, a previous desire gone to worms. All conceptions predetermine their degeneration or supersedure by degrees of morality. Verily a new sexuality shall be mine,-unnecessary to degenerate or surpass. To give it a name, I call it the Unmodified sexuality; without a name it shall be conscious of all desire: thus no ecstasy shall escape me. Its wisdom shall be dreams of Self-love vibrating all the manifestations-I am he, who self pleasures non-morally."

The Dead Body of Aaos

Aaos preparing for death uttered in soliloque:

"O, thou inconceivableness that transcends human desire; thou magnificent incongruous Face. For millions of years thou hast not wearied of my body. What would Thy pleasure be but for my wantonness?" "I teach you the glad death of all things." Thus spake my knowing mouth. "My belief has created the more beautiful body and desires of rebirth. Fear I the transvaluation called death? Knew I not death, when time was born? Arise, old memory! And tell my consciousness of this frequent experience-once again!" Then Death spake unto Aaos: "No stranger, nor enemy to me is Aaos, we are too ancient friends to come to blows. What hast thou come to take from me this time? What fresh associations for thy new body? No self-denial has Aaos! Thou hast not come to rap tables. To awake the disembodied Astrals!" Aaos answered: "In my life my memory lived numerous remotenesses which were once me. My belief reached associations that out-stripped all morality and rationalism. My I chanced much with the Self: certain it is, I come not to repent . . nor seek a wife. Yea, my will conquered faith and sincere-

[140]

ly laughed at every righteousness! Now that my individual consciousness dissolves, to saturate again with its furthermost desires, to form the new body: -O mighty death, remember at the time of incarnating- my utmost immorality, my frightening madnesses, my jesting sins, my satyr carouses, my grotesque concubine of chaos! Remember O death, my frenzied longing that has no name [Oh, forget my first kiss of love, now withered as a fallen leaf]. Make this my sexuality complete, all knowing, so that I may again procreate the lusty Self-love in isolation!" Then Aaos spake unto the ferryman: "O time, of nothing now am I ashamed to admit parentage. What I generate is future, body to become. I have learned and unlearned in equal labouring this universe. Hard has been my faith and denial. That which is incomprehensible have I made,- have I impelled inwards to make secure for reaction. My knowledge is but the murmuring of a few words with ever changing intonation and meaning. For I have suffered that which shall never be forgotten or spoken: Thus much have I realized of Life. Where is fear when I impel procreation? O earth! all memories! solid, liquid, vapour and flaming! Old sentiment is my body, germinating afresh: again to exist and change by the command, 'I desire.' The Alpha and Omega of my wisdom is-glad suicide: it has become inevitable and shall be my payment to thee. Steel and poison are my friends. Steel for Self, poison for vermin-for myself diseased. I will this fruitful violence, my death kiss, thus to realize my hyper-commands." With his belief firmly fixed, his full red lips smiling, with bright eyes; Aaos clasped his sword saying: "Greater love hath no man than Self-destruction in pleasure." No new experience for Aaos! And thus he died.

Death is named the great unknown. Assuredly, death is the great chance. An adventure in will, that translates into body. What happens after death? Will it be more surprising than this world? Could I say? My experience may not be the commonplace . . . Without doubt, all shall experience the 'rushing winds' that blow from within, the body beyond perspective, into cosmic dust,-till consciousness again develops. Death is a transfiguration of life, an inversion, a reversion of the consciousness to parentage and may be a diversion! A continuation of evolution. The coming forth of the suppressed. Do you know what happens to the body at death? Exactly what changes take place? Well, so it happens to your beliefs, desires, etc., that make consciousness, for all things seen are incarnate desire, the unseen; Ideas of the past and future bodies. From these the new body is determined and parentage selected by the laws of attraction. The wise man makes sure of his future parents and a male incarnation before death. Consciousness [for most, only three dimensions] is not so definite as in life but to the extent of your will in life, that much is your consciousness in death. Death is the manufacture of life. A dream is a sore likeness of Life. Death is a sore dream of life. Its period depending on the perfection or otherwise of the individual but closely follows in duration the previous life-till re-incarnation. Death being a living nightmare of life, has painful possibilities-in the degree of unified consciousness. A ghostly world of 'perhaps' where all the vague potentialities of desire, are incarnating. There is no women as such. Again I say, death is the great chance and there grasp where thou hast before failed in body. If fate is life, then death is the hazard to alter fate! A world where will creates the afterthought in its own image. For most, death will hold mainly blank pages, but were we ever treated all alike? Study your dreams in this life, it may help you in the death posture.

Spare [143]

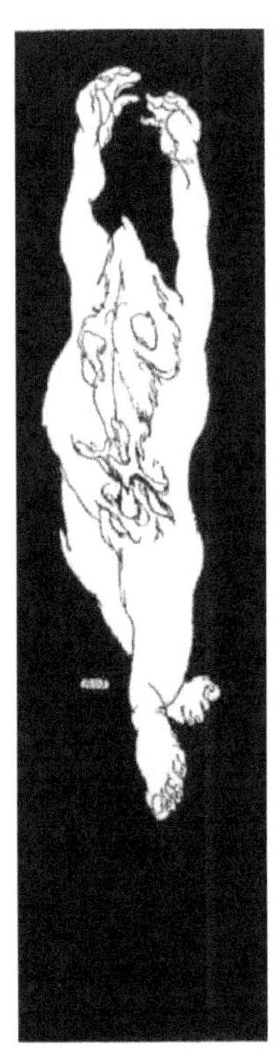

The Death Posture

The Heaven of Aaos

"All things are subject to resurrection" thus spake smiling Aaos, on rising from the dead. Then turning towards his shadow . . . . "I come! the changing word that destroys religion, a vortex wind that shall jest in Temples! Again! A reveller in the marshalled order of the sexes, the mad anarch of desires, the wild satyr of wolfish kisses! Once again to earth, O Thou whirlwind of desire, thou drunken breath of ribald lightning! My vampire chalice of ecstasy! Yea, as my rapacious flame reareth before thee, thou escapeth from me with the laughing whisper of thy wonderful pleasure! O, L.C.O' CS!! thou insatiable thirst of my self-love, with none but thee will I procreate!" "What now am I after resurrection? The sinful despair of magic? I am the Iconoclast of Logos: The sun-satyr of Chaos! Thunder and lightnings? Yea, a vital gaiety to drowsy dust, to blase souls. Ecstatic laughter that reverberates and awakens . . . I am the shuddering heights and suffocating depths of ego, slipping and becoming. Inconceivable women am I. A clouded vista of abyss, wherein to visit naked, my vampire Self. Wherein to write a cryptic language of my sexes, that I am the Key. Wherein to belch forth venomous atmosphere towards the highest. Wherein to drench my thirsted tongue on thy goat's milk; to battle with thy cataleptic kisses, to swoon in thy consuming subtilty. O my mistress, I am unutterably drunk striving thy depths. I am the great cypher of love and hate knotted. The sphinx surviving, never sufficiently imagined. I am the grotesque refractions of form and Self. The bitter purgative, called death. A violence that out-lasts the morning. Moon turbulent waters am I: the frightening black Albatross of un-ashamed women-where men are. I am the over mature breasts of a child: the virgin womb, hidden by nightmares. Constant in metamorphosis, permeating creation without compassion. The unexcelled impulse that has never failed. Yea, I am all these-yet never known. My kiss is a sword thrust! For whom, am I, this insatiable fountain in the hot deserts? Only for thee, O, L.C.O'CS!" Thus sang Aaos, the blasphemer, throwing off his grave shroud. Going again among men [for he pleasured in all men], he gave unto them his magic book, named: "Life and Death, the jest called love, wherein every man is a God, in whatsoever he will his belief." And Aaos passed his way, muttering to his goatish beard: "What now is left all hope is dead? For I have buried my illusion and dishonesty. Thus my body is now all inconceivableness! O, God, where is thine enemy?"

The Dreams of Aaos

The I and the Arcanum:

One day the time drew near for the experiment and Aaos was watching the waters, to make arcana by arbitrary projection into the utter void of his isolation. And this was his wish-"In future my dreams shall interpretate themselves as will [i.e. reaction]." For, he reasoned: "Why not live asleep all suffering?" Aaos had lived the preliminary ritual of habit in the cesspools and exhausted them in the mountains. Before projection he prayed thus to the waters:-"O thou I, vice versa-my God. I at least shall not be thy jest. In life I have realized possibilities not contained in heaven-amidst a cowardice inconceivable but accomplished everywhere. I have made known [opening his book] something that is different to the muck of retouched photography which men call reality: although it has been the evil habit of thousands of years. I have created art [lived belief] that surpasses all evolved conception. I have incarnated that which I-need to rationalize: Verily-not the ever present portraiture of experience to satisfy the ovine: No obvious allegory of asses-thinking God: No still-life group of empty bottles and old maids commonplaces: Nor the gay-tragedy of song. But strange desires of stranger arcana. The law I make while thinking God-and will smash and remake again: so that I may commit every conceivable sin against its word. My utility has been-my pleasure-that alone is my service to man and to heaven, in that I am the Goat." After his devotion Aaos prepared for the Death posture and judgement. Awaking from the awful wrath-his teeth chattering, his limbs shivering and drenched with a cold perspiration, he allowed the ague to exhaust itself and thought thus: "Verily, I have nothing to forgive or repent . . . Alas! what fears this I but its own conditions? Man will create the faster moving body outside himself-always prefering compulsion to the infinite possibilities of freedom.

Alas! Alas! that which is ornamental reacts its uselessness-the symbol 'I was.' The necrologue of love-is utility." Then rising from his couch and taking an ecstatic inbreath: "Again would I die violently and jest at God." The operation having exhausted him he suffered this daydream: "The waters became murky, then muddy, and movement began. Going nearer, he observed-a phosphorescent morass crowded with restless abortions of humanity and creatures-like struggling mudworms, aimless and blind: an immense swamp of dissatisfaction; a desire smashed into pieces." With his will, the dream changed and he became in a vast warehouse-cum-brothel. Realizing his whereabouts he muttered: "Such

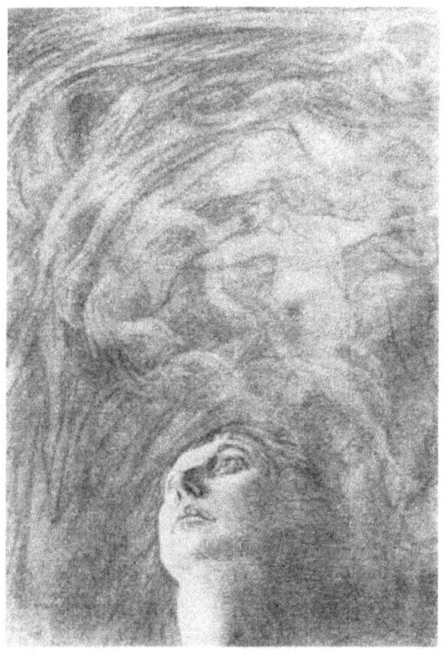

Aaos was watching the waters

is life, an endless swallowing and procreation, morally, man is a bastard." The floor was strewn with dirty clothes and candle ends: knowing the strangest women, nothing was pleasing enough ...so his attention wandered to the upper story. He was certain he had been there before by a staircase. But now, there was no easy means of access. He would have to climb whatever served. After much painful effort he managed to reach and hang on to the balustrade of the upper floor. There, he noticed the store contained innumerable strange effigies and new creations of humanity. He struggled further along to obtain an easy means of ingress, thinking: "Where there is desire-there shall be found the desired sleeping partner. What is true, is pleasurable Self. I have now reached the sixth letter of the alphabet." When suddenly he observed another and more agile following him-who when reaching Aaos, clutched hold of him-shouting: "Where I cannot reach, thou too shall not ascend." Their combined weight became too heavy-the balustrading collapsed and they both fell . . . Aaos felt himself falling as into a bottomless pit-when with a start he awoke, and after introspection spoke to his heart: "Verily I have fallen in love with a new belief and become moral! This I re-

flects itself differently. What was once easy- is
now difficult. All reflections are radiated matter
incarnating. Who doth know what his own still-
ness refracts at the time of its projection? Who
would suspect afterthought without conscious-
ness? The I, to be self prophecy-without a con-
glomeration of old clothes-is by a deliberation
previous to will-to be noumenal; is anterior to
time. Forgive? [i.e. to free from consciousness].
Yea, a thousand times! so that the desire be-
come large and insane enough to self-will. How
can memory forget-when we invented reaction?
What is all bad memory-but morality? What is
will but reaction-impulsed from the accidents of
I?" Then Aaos remembered he had conditioned
his realization by thought of time and remarked:
"So ends in the part sexuality-all asses' magic
that premeditates time. Much thought destroys
the nerve. The arcana knows more than the
I wills: and thus should I have it." Then Aaos
laughed aloud and spoke: "Up! Up! my sexuality!
and be a light unto all-that is in me!" For he had-
while contemplating-eluded his I and knew he
would shortly obtain . . . And thus he found a
new use for his righteousness.

Self-Love and Map Making

Aaos in his youth had many dreams, pleasing and otherwise; awake and in his sleep. Frequently, fragments of dreams haunted him for many a day, but they were of his marriage bed. After his divorce he slept alone with his sword. Aaos, once dreamed he was till asleep, and this was his dream: "He had been exploring an unknown country and having returned, was busy making maps from his rough sketches and memoranda. He was surprised how fresh was his memory of every questioned detail, at the ease with which his hand drew the mountains and contours of that unknown country. His dexterity became too pleasing and threatened an event long ceased and then forgotten." By his determination he awoke and was able to calm the excited passion. He was consoled that nothing had happened. Then he spoke to himself thus: "What new deceit is this? Must I be for ever solving the changing symbolism of the wretched morality-called 'I'? Do I still need a loin cloth for my passions? Verily, to be alone and map drawing is now an unsafe art! Sleep?-This sexual excitement still obtains. Procreation is with more things than women. The function of the sexuality is not entirely procreation: stranger experiences are promised than ever imagination conceived! One must retain-to give birth to will. Behold! my Self-love, thee I pleasure too well,-to let slip into other being!"

Aaos and the Undertaker

One dark night, leaving the tavern more or less sober and wandering without thought, I arrived at a well illuminated undertaker's shop. Intoxicated, I am always curious of the work in such places-so here I paused. At that moment, the door was flung violently open and five drunken undertaker's assistants lurched into me. I objected in a mild way, they being numerous and I thinking that drunkards are lucky . . . But that any resistance or excuses I might offer would be unsatisfactory was too apparent. They had reached the quarrelsome state and I discovered-I knew these men too well! From argument to foul accusations [and what did they not call me?]-came blows-I thought it safer not to run away. Did I fight well? I know they did and with drunken humour dragged me into the shop to purchase a coffin. Within, came recognition-Alas, too truly they knew me! From then no quarter was given. That drunken fight among the dead and funeral furniture was hopeless for me. I was robbed, stripped, spat upon, kicked and bound-what abuse did I not suffer? I think the humiliation and blows rendered me unconscious! But, I was not to rest so easily-they soon brought me back to consciousness for worse things . . . And I was told they had recently finished making my wife's coffin. They then forced me to view her dead body. Even in my pitiable state, I thought of the beauty of her corpse. Again, they reviled me because of her: she who, if I had not neglected her, would still be living. I, the whoremonger, betrayer of women, and arch-abnormalist. After much other insult; they told me-my fate. I was given the choice of being burnt to death or buried alive with her! Naturally my choice was to be alone. But no such chance was to be mine. I was buried alive with her corpse. With their combined weight forcing on the lid. I thought I was dead [for did I not hear the rushing winds?] when doubt crept into my soul. Then realization of life dawned when I felt that cold corpse crushed against my body by the tightness of the coffin,-never have I realized such horror! With a mighty yell, my after suspiration burst that overcrowded coffin into fragments! I arose, thinking I was alone. But no, sitting by the corpse, amid the debris was-the

[154]

devil grinning! To be alone and half alive with the devil is not a welcome anti-climax ... Then he spoke unto me: "Coward! where was thy courage, even against drunken enemies? Ah ah! Thou hast indeed willed pleasure! Who has the power, Thou or I? What medicine for the dead Gods! Thou wretched scum of littlenesses-heal thy gaping wounds, thou art more fitted to pray than to prey." Much more did he utter, till my very ears closed. With a body torn to pieces, crushed in every part-what was I to answer? My silence compelled him again to speak: "Hast thou no complaint?" In a mighty rage-for this was a worse goad than all my earlier suffering-I answered: "Curses, no! keep your possessions.-I will pleasure. Do your utmost! this poor thing my body you will again replace!" Then I fought the devil and behold,-I became alone! What happened? I, in my miserable plight, not even my teeth left-how could I have conquered the devil? Did I become a succubus? Perhaps-I became the devil? But this I know-I did will pleasure. And from this day shall smile into all men's faces.

Then Aaos awoke and murmured: "Belief and desire are the great duality which engender all illusions that entangle the senses [i.e. sexual-

ity] and prevent free will. What is all acciden-
tal suffering but reaction from dead loves now
become diableries. How much are we sensible
of body? Yet the composition of the body is its
relationship between consciousness and all cre-
ation. Without doubt I am now an-undertaker!"

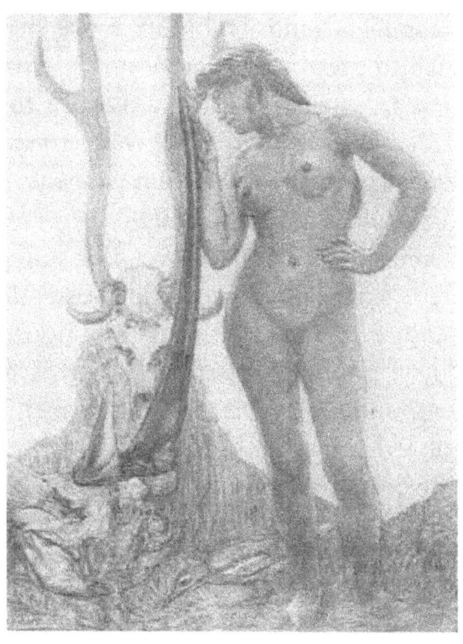

Tzula

The Death of Tzula

In his sleep Aaos one day met his sister Tzula and learned she was thinking of marriage and she questioned him thus: "My most loved brother, what is your opinion of entering marriage? I would be guided by your experience and cunning on sexual matters. My body is weak from desire and suffers a horrible restlessness that surprises my habits of virginity." Aaos answered: "What cause is there for astonishment? This life force acts and invents from itself; even when the usual channels of expression are open. How much more so-when closed and the nature non-moral? With deceivers, one may well promise and not fulfil for this end, that with a double will there shall be satisfaction without the labour of birth. Resist not desire by repression: but tranmute desire by changing to the greater object." Tzula answered: "Alas! this dreadful thing of desire seeks its liberation in willing opposite to all my efforts of conciliation: Cannot marriage be my emancipation?" Aaos answered: "O my sister, must thou become ever smaller from thy small desires? Oh! renounce half-desiring, much better is it to marry the evil. For thee my sister, I wish no marriage but the marriage of the greater love. For I announce, the day to come, yea it is nigh, thy absorption in a male incarnation. What is nature but thy past will incarnated and removed from consciousness by its further desires? The relationship still living provokes the involuntary purpose-thy opposition to which causes disease, and is but resistance of the I to the Self. Bind thy desire by attention on Thy love of desire-lest it wholly runs away. Prevent thy belief from incarnating through this consciousness of the ever present greater desire. Forestall the inclinations of desire by this and not by other means of exhausting desire. Neither abstinence nor over indulgence necessarily destroys. Verily, my sister I would have thee a male incarnation." Then he became sleepy his sister becoming dim and the dream more meaningless, till he felt something that made him start with horror-awaking he perceived someone leave his couch! Aaos seizing his sword gnashing his teeth, trembling in every limb, and with ghastly visage, shouted: "Alpha and Omega! Thou thyself shall throttle that which thou wouldst surpass," And swung his sword which struck horribly . . . Then shaking the perspiration from his head he muttered to himself; "Verily! again am I the pitiable moralist, the drowsiest of watchman. Sisters were ever deceivers! All virgins are foolish; What does their virginity matter?" Then clasping his sword again he went to his couch and tried to rest but no sleep came, until daybreak: for he wondered who his sister was.

The Butcher of Those Who Follow

In a dream, Aaos one day crossed the border line and wandered into the flat country towards what seemed, in the half-rain, a deserted heap of ruins. Arriving closer to the city, there issued from it a dreadful stench accompanying agonizing groans. Entering the gates Aaos found it a vast slaughterer's abattoir; an endless shambles of dying bodies tied in sacks. The black mud of the streets was streaming blood, the carnal houses bespattered-the very atmosphere pulsating agony; the grey sky reflecting its red. Holding his nose and stopping his ears Aaos walked on . . . Then he paused and his frightened eyes watched the work of slaughter and he observed that every victim was already beheaded, but not dead, that they were sheep and being bled to death. As he watched the mass of writhing corpses in that foul Bedlam of death groans—made more loathsome by the ribald jesting of the slaughtermen, the scene became more vast, more heathenly impossible, when he noticed towering before him a giant shape with gory sheepskin used as loincloth, who, with a shrill voice shouted: "Woe unto you that seek this awful place of satiety. I am the guardian named Necrobiosis, in order that there may be mobility!" Then seeing Aaos he laughed hideously, and addressed him thus: "But why cometh Aaos in the close season? Thou old dodger of Time, thou eye winking at all things! For thou canst will love in that which is most repulsive. Away O Aaos, Thou too art an arch-slaughterer of sheep. " Then the giant gave an awful grimace and turned his back, snapping his teeth and howling like a dog. Becoming larger and larger till of cosmic vastness, thus he disappeared. When Aaos awoke, he muttered to himself: "Beyond time there is a sensation as of awaking from the utmost impossibility of existence from the mad dreams we call reality; the stupidities we call will." Then Aaos arose to fill his lungs with fresh air and have the good of motion.

On the Announcer of Great Events

One night, Aaos dreamed he was mournfully labouring his way uphill, through an endless ruin of cities. The streets were a chaos of debris-the air heavy with the stale stench of damp charred wood and mouldeing refuse. No-where saw he a sign of life-The sky was dead and breathless. Stumbling along till his body sickened. Wearily he paused to rest and looking down, noticed the litter of a manuscript. Stooping, he chose the nearest fragment, and this was what he read: "I too was once a mighty pleasure garden of all things that enchanted the sense s; possessing men and women of every desirable form and nationality. All the hidden treasures of nature were exhibited with art and cunning accident. No desire could be ungratified. . . . What am I now? A putrid mess and dust of dead habitations. An empty wineskin destroyed and gone rotten! O, stranger, what is the cause of my desolation?" Aaos, sitting down, mused long to himself: "When the very ground beneath one's feet collapses, what is secure? What chance of escape- but fore-knowledge? Would the study of grammar, or correct pronounciation of language, save one?" While he was thus meditating, suddenly he was afraid and gave a start. For beside his shadow grew another shadow. And when he looked round, there stood before him an illuminated youth who said: "Awake Aaos, This sorry ruin thou didst cause by thy greater love. All these pleasures were but dreams, which awoke too violently. What is all sexuality but the infinite synonyms of Self-love; self created and destroyed? These pleasures now dead, suppressed their own antecedent indulgence by after-thoughts of women. All original thought, once suppressed becomes volcanic." Aaos, winking his eye, answered: "When asleep, one should procreate in barren soil?" at which they both smiled. After they had surveyed each other, Aaos arose and left the youth. Surmounting an eminence he searched the sky long, until he observed the faint glow of the sun struggling through the mists, he spake thus: "Abstinence from righteousness by total indiscrimination, becomes limitlessness. O Sun! like thee, I too will kiss all things and sleep alone, so that they propagate my ecstasy!" Awaking Aaos remembered his purpose, and spoke to his heart: "The arcana of desire [i.e. Self-love] would be satisfied with none but its original Self-by the unique. Thus my morality taught me by dream symbols. As in life, so in sleep-all things have a sexual significance, hidden by righteousness. Herein is a mystery and the means to will. What is all humanity but one's own forgotten deliberation-becoming restless? The unexpected bark of a dog should not frighten. Neither is medicine taken by pronouncing the name of the remedy. Verily, in the time of cataclysm it is too late to pick the right word."

The Dream That Came True

One night Aaos was pleasured with this dream:

In his early youth, he met a beautiful maiden-famous among men who knew perfection. She was everything desirous, even to her name. He became her lover, and knew her . . . to be true. But an evil voice spoke unto him and he doubted her, believing the voice-because it was of one he had made his friend. In youth-like rage he cast aside his lover and wandered into marriage of every kind, without satisfaction. Then the evil voice died. For years Aaos wandered restlessly seeking, but never finding his lost love: thinking they were both in Hell. Then in his utmost weariness and despair, he thought much more deeply; and at last realized that the dream was the time for magic. And then he willed . . . With the new moon his wish was materialized and again he met his first and only love. Their hearts being still virgin, Aaos spoke unto her: "Out of Chaos have I awaked and found thee, O beloved. Death itself shall not part us; for by thee alone will I have children." And they mar-

ried and were ecstatic thereafter: for in their ec-
stasy he noticed Death smile. Aaos then awoke
still living their ecstasy, and breathing heavily,
spake to him self thus: "When the thing desired
is again incarnated at the time of ecstasy; there
can be no satiety. ONE! we now part. All things
are possible with the original belief, once again
found. The belief, simultaneous with the desire,
becomes its parallel and duality ceases. When
ecstasy is transcended by ecstasy, the I becomes
atmospheric-there is no place for sensuous ob-
jects to conceive differently and react. Verily,
greater will has no man than to-jest in ecstasy:
retain thyself from giving forth thy seed of life."
Aaos rising from his couch-threw away his sword
and exclaimed aloud: "Now for reality!"

THE FORMULAE OF ZOS VEL THANATOS

FIRST FORMULA:
Of the White Sabbath— as first told me by a Witch

Argument

Actually there is neither a Black nor a White Sabbath: the ethical criterion of all acts is whether they are anti-social or so motivated. Where two or more of a kind of equal maturity and inclination enact for consummation, then, if harm they do it is only to themselves–which I doubt–and far less harmful than the practices of those who mutilate or deny their bodies in the name of a culture or a religion. The latter are invariably prophets or propagators of sterility, whereas the one outward tenet of Witchcraft is silence to "unlike others".

The Sabbath is an inverse-reversion for self-seduction, an undoing for a divertive conation. Sex is used as the technique and medium of

a magical act. There is not only erotic satisfac-
tion; the sensualist is made detached and con-
trolled until final sublimation; his whole training
is submissive and obedient until, by cold amor-
al passion, he can transmute control and divert
him- or herself where desired.

The Witch so engaged is old, grotesque,
worldly and libidinously learned and is sexual-
ly attractive as a corpse; yet she becomes the
entire vehicle of consummation. This is nec-
essary to transmute the personal aesthetic cul-
ture. Perversion is used only to overcome moral
prejudices or conformity; the mind and desire
must become amoral, focused and made entirely
acceptive so that the life-force is free of inhi-
bitions prior to the control. Thus, the Sabbath
becomes a deliberate sex-orgy for the purpose
of materialization: the Great Reality of 'as if'
(wishful thinking). Sex is fully exploited: he who
injures none, himself does not injure.

Finally: a culturally accepted criterion has
destroyed more affective affinity than any oth-
er belief; but he who transmutes the ugly into
a new aesthetic has something beyond fear. For
the ethical pragmatist I can assert that this for-
mula has never harmed me; on the contrary, by
improved health and self-control it has made me

tolerant, understanding and compassionate. It inspires and promises more than probability as possible, and is the only thing that has made reality magical and the magical, reality. Pleasure is in us and around us... now I beckon and it cometh unto me.

Formula

This is always secret, communal and periodic; an enforced consummation for almost unlimited wish-fulfillment by lengthy voluntary abstinence, repression and sacrifice until release by mass sexual saturation, for one purpose: the exteriorization of a wish by a great saving and a total spending.

The hypereroticism induced by this grand-scale hysteria or saturnalia has an essentially sado-masochistic basis. Previous to the ceremony each celebrant has his or her allotted part, although it usually ends promiscuously and chaotically. The initiates are trained singly in their own parts and in the response expected of them. They play a passive role, for the promise of untold ecstasy. The Witches take the active part throughout: thus the symbolic levitation by besom-handle.

There is a meeting-place and an elaborate ritual which is an extensive hypnotic to override all inhibitions. Thus, smell, hearing and vision are seduced by incense and mantra (incantation and the ritual-ceremony), while taste and touch are enhanced by the stimuli of wine and oral acts. After complete sexual satiation by oral, anal, or urethral means, there appears an exteriorized hallucination of the predetermined wish which is magical in its reality. No one can say precisely whether certain things happen or not, although each person may have very different and equally vivid experiences. Some form of levitation seems common to all. My own experience of many Sabbaths is that there is consummate exteriorization and that subsequent memories are of reality.

All excessively sadistic acts are usually symbolized by genuine Witches, but what simulation there is is common to most erotic rights. The whole ceremony is based mainly on inverted orthodox religious services.

Doctrine and Credo

'Fornicatus benedictus! Almighty Ashmodeus, existent of Chaos, ominous by thy name, thy kingdom come through me on earth. Lead me into all temptations of my flesh so I may trespass greatly into thy ways by my desires: for thou art all sex-seeking unity, thou mighty genitalia of creation that knoweth no satiation—grant thou my wish, for thou art all power, ecstasy and actuality. Amen!'

A small talisman arabesque of the major erotic zones is passed around and kissed by all. Then follows a short perverse communion, then a symposium with suggestive exhibitionism, libidinous stories and abreaction of sexual fantasies—developing into the real thing.

SYNOPSIS OF THE SABBATH

Theory of Formula

Differentiation is the stimulus of recreation, hence perversions and contra-practices are used to that end. Ceremony and Ritual are the matrices of form and order, the thesis being that by the act of 'as if' the wish is fleshed when magically charged. The act of exuviations is by transference to the powers of elemental automata as delegated by the obsessive mind. Thus reality may obtain, and for a while serve its own purpose. The ecstatic moment is used as the fecund instant of wish-endowment; for at that period of reality, the Will, Desire, and Belief are aligned and in unison. Faith is a form of compulsory autohypnosis which may build up and enter belief. The great believers have no need of faith–and we are all convinced by the flesh of things.

The Affirmation Creed

I believe: 'I become the potentialities where I made effort... the funambulatory way between ecstasies: The acceptance of all things, in entering all doors and the by-passing: Unto myself only the law I make–the good and evil I affirm: The relatability of all things to ego, the apotheosis of Knowledge in ecstasy: In the Gods and eternal flesh as all truth: That my way is the only way for me, however devious: That... which I have enveloped from me, shall come forth as a potent elemental to my aid.

And I believe without reservation in the preservation of my concepts as the media of Ego, from which all things ultimately become. Amen.'

Prayer of Communion

We who are about to partake of each other, shall walk past all amorous sickness and deaths, for we are within the magical equinox.

Amen

We who proudly make unto ourselves every graven image, shall have great copulations and are allowed to love our Gods, for we know the Sacred Alignments.

Amen

We who do not crucify—nothing shall hurt us that is of the 'Nature'; neither our comings and goings from the womb, for we have the Key to all aesthetics.

Amen

In this sacred moment (here occurs the symbolic eating of flesh and blood) we forget our enemies: therefore let our dead children sleep. And let our dead loves arise, so they too may watch and enjoy our ecstasies. Let their animation be power to our memories and so resurge all ecstasy, for in this day there shall be no inhibitions.

Amen

Thou insatiable peripheral quadriga of sex.

Amen

Prayer of Adoration

Thou lambent spirit of Erh!

Thou hast kindled the sacred fire from dead ashes, so my torch lightens all darknesses.

Thou hast become the fulcrum of my will.

Everlastingly in Thee I know not respite:

Except in the sensuous impact of flesh, there are no meanings.

Thou hast awakened me into eternities.

Thou makest all things beautiful unto the grotesque.

Whom thou succour hath no sterility.

I am reborn and reborn into desirous becomings:

I have recreated my Soul by birthing pleasure.

Through Thee my will, desire, belief and word become the law

That carries me into the Catastrophic beyond becoming:

Thou the emissary of Neither-Neither!

Ever Silent Watcher! Thou hast shown me the new sexualities

And all the mysteries of the Threshold!

Only Thee I adore in my Soul and my everlasting body.

Alpha-Omega–Amen!

Evocation

O mighty Rehctaw!

Thou who exists in all erogenousnesses

We evoke Thee!

By the power of the meanings arising from
these forms I make
    We evoke Thee!
    By the Talismans that speak the secret leit-
motif of desire
    We evoke Thee!
    By the sacrifices, abstinences and transvalu-
ations we make
    We evoke Thee!
    By the sacred inbetweenness concepts
    Give us the flesh!
    We, who shall suffer all ecstasies
    Give us the will!
    By the quadriga sexualis
    Give us invariant desire!
    By the conquest of fatigue
    Give us eternal resurgence!
    By the most sacred Word-graph
    We invoke Thee.
    Amen

SECOND FORMULA:
The Formula of Plotinus— as sent to me through the Delphic Pythoness via Automatism, called "Giving life to the Autistic by Virgin Earthenware"

(Now unto this period I had copulated only the atmosphere or rode whores, lined old hags, witches and bitches of all kinds, there being few virgins.)

The autotelic wish into heterotelic conception is by concummation through using an urn of correct shape and dimension which must correlate nearly to that of the lingam used—so that there is sufficient vacuum. At the moment of orgasm the wish must be imperatively stated. After ejaculation seal the vase with your sigil and with the secret formula of your desire. Bury same at midnight, the moon being quartered. When the moon wanes, disinter and pour contents as libation into earth with suitable incantation, and re-bury same. This is the most formidable formula known, never fails and is dangerous—hence what is not written must be guessed. From this formula was derived the legend of the Genii of the Brazen Vessel as related by Solomon.

[176]

THIRD FORMULA:
The Communion of
Auto-Ego to Zos

This formula is based on that of Apollonius the Pythagorean philosopher and theurgist, and is the only magical means of inseparation and psychic help that has no disastrous aftereffects whether it fails or succeeds.

There is nothing simpler than speaking to your inmost self, and nothing more difficult. The first conditions are Secrecy, Silence and Solitude. Next, a means of communication: I created my own Alphabet and Language based on the primal onomatopoeia of language which is now—for me—a subconscious quality which expresses only by high emotionalism. Indeed, the active link between all images of thought are intro-audile and of this character on which one's psychic language must be based. The Soul responds to the basic language only. Finally, ease of body and mind must obtain, the mind being free from all concepts—except the Desire, which should be altruistic (others or yourself). Your request should be as brother asking brother in words worthy to reach your greater self. You will receive only what you are fitted to receive.

FOURTH FORMULA:
How to return Evil to its Source

Sorcery may be good or evil, as predetermined by its purpose, and is your responsibility. Corrective punishment, being amoral, is the only legitimate motivation. Ability is the determining factor of success.

Sufficient hate is the potency, which must be stored up, formulated and focused so as to become incarnate through the elemental employed to pierce the protective aura of the offenders. Requisites: something personal belonging to the victim or victims. A symbolic replica of them (drawing, statuette, etc.). Also, the deployment of an animal familiar, and a simulation of the deed and desired consequences formulated as a ritual convincing to yourself.

There is also a direct method by suggestion, when knowing the offenders' 'Achilles Heel'. Evil in others may be made potent against them.

FIFTH FORMULA:
Of Fortune Telling by Cards
(Foretelling by Familiars)

Foretelling the future by cards or other means: What is of consequence, and portentous, is the 'state of mind' that is induced in the consultant by the method and downright explanations given to him: there is an indirect or transposed auto-suggestion. Anything so entering the near-subconscious must reformulate and re-suggest itself with commitment to a later, similar, event. Likewise, the sorcerer's shaft pierces through the protective aura by assertion becoming indirect suggestion as the consultant's own. Paradoxically, the quickest way of susceptibility is by denial as disbelief.

Cards may be used for formulating the will, casting spells, mathematical numerology, and fortune telling. I was taught quite early in life by the greatest Witch of recent years. Here is a rough synopsis of my formula based on what I remember of hers.

First I need certain conditions: Silence, and light just sufficient to work by. I even close my eyes when shuffling and always do so before handing the cards to the querent for re-shuffling.

To begin with I used ordinary playing cards but soon found it expedient and of greater service to make my own packs, using sixty cards. Divided as usual into four suits, the Court cards representing people. The different suits represent the common factors of life, i.e., business, social relations, objects, events, and emotional qualities, etc., no individual card having itself much significance. I am giving only general principles; I shall not repeat what may be gleaned from a summary of books on the subject. Events and all else are given importance, in degree, by simple or more complex combinations of similar or relating cards. Illustration: The two of Spades means simply 'slight indisposition'; the nine of Spades means 'annoyance' or 'pain'; the ten of Spades means 'sorrow'. Thus, these cards in that order mean 'serious illness'. If the card representing the enquirer is there, it means their own illness, and with the card representing 'fatality' for good or evil (reverse or otherwise), it could mean death.

A different arrangement or sequence of the same cards would give a different equivalent, extended meaning, or definition. Thus, the two of Spades isolated from similar cards could mean 'slight illness', 'faintheartedness', or 'reluctance' etc., depending on which other cards it 'falls' against. The cards should not be too ambiguous and should become definite and different by combination. This is sufficient information for beginning to create the 'meanings' of cards, the only difficulty being to give appropriate meanings to individual cards so as to have a complete vocabulary capable of covering all exigencies. Start with what you can manage and build up by constant addition and rectification. Combinations are endless—always make them rational. The more rare the event, the greater the number of cards necessary to the combination. It takes months of work to create a really rational pack. Start with playing cards, writing your meaning on them. Later, make your own pack and draw your own symbols—geometrical shapes will serve. Be original—it gives the best results. My own four cards mentioned above:

Methods of laying out cards are numerous. The best, for general prediction, is serpentine: reading from left to right in rows of nine cards.

Synopsis: I do a short horoscope by laying eleven rows of five cards, each row relating to: House, Love, Self, etc.,—every four rows being relative to each other... and answer to wish. The five cards left over indicate the immediate event. Make your own rules and keep them, consistency in this case being a great virtue.

It is possible to predict anything, but special packs with their special meanings have to be made, a difficult and laborious task.

ALTERNATE FIFTH FORMULA:
Technique of Fortune Telling

First obtain a good book on 'fortune telling' by playing cards. This will give you a general idea for the making a suitable pack for your own purposes. Procure a pack of ordinary playing cards and mark them, top and bottom (cards have a reverse). Rely on the 'book' only for general direction and method–the remnants of a traditional and lost art. You should evolve your own meanings, symbols and methods. This is vital. Here are the salient points to note:

Individual cards are indicators, not events–at least, not the important ones, and so we make separate cards mean the small commonplaces–emotions and abstracts (love, hate, fear, etc.); 'people' are indicated by the Kings and Queens, and 'children' by the two Knaves. The different suits symbolize the different kinds of events or emotions, etc. Thus, Spades relate to sickness, mourning, death, disappointment, fear, hatred. Hearts indicate love, marriage, friendship, happiness, generosity. Diamonds indicate money, success, fame, honour. Clubs indicate business, officialism, power, knowledge.

You will find fifty-two cards more than adequate to cover the small meanings. There are a number of meanings that do not fall under any one suit in particular, such as 'speedy', 'accidental', 'legal', etc.; these should be placed in any suit where there is room. Put similar meanings on one card, such as 'conclusion' and 'death'. The reverse of a card means the same thing but more intensely or extensively. Thus: 'slight sickness', reversed, would mean 'real sickness'. Also, a special card is made to intensify any card it falls against; reversed it means 'continuous' or 'regular'.

It is the combination of certain cards that indicates the meanings of the more important events and episodes of life. For example: a combination of Spades—'Nine', 'Ten', and 'Ace'—when so closely juxtaposed would mean death very soon and, in combination with cards meaning 'accident', 'sickness', 'hate', would mean death by accident, sickness, murder or suicide, and so on, covering every possible event.

The mathematical computations of fifty-two cards are almost limitless. Write your meanings and principal combinations on the cards, and when you have fully memorized them change them into symbols—even if your imagination cannot suggest more than geometrical signs. This change to symbols is very important. To save overloading the cards with writing or symbols, write down a list of the rarer combinations and their meanings. Study (from books on fortune-telling) the different methods of laying out the cards for reading; ultimately you will evolve the method that suits you best.

My method is simply to lay them out in a line (or four lines of thirteen cards) and read from left to right, but it is difficult and only adepts succeed. This is my process:

First the operator must shuffle the cards whilst looking into the eyes of the querent. The pack is then passed to the querent with a request to shuffle whilst thinking about whatever he desires to know. Then lay out the cards and read, special note being made of the juxtapositions of combinations. When close together it means the event will occur soon.

However many combinations there are you

will always find some of unique and baffling meaning, and this is where the actual skill of the operator comes in. The solving of the problem(s) will be found far more interesting than any crossword puzzle. Imaginative methods help. A simple illustration:

One card means 'fear' and the other 'honour'. This could be read as meaning that the person in question is 'fainthearted' but has the necessary ability, as against 'he fears for his honour'—if it does not seem to be implied by other factors.

Remember, there is a rational and true interpretation if you can find it. Whether you believe in the subject or not it should be apprehended as you would approach any other Art or Science—with an open mind. As to the attitude of the querent, his belief is immaterial but he should be willing to be unprejudiced; any facetiousness is fatal. I can assert—judging by the results of others who have used this method—that any person of normal intelligence who follows carefully these suggestions and who uses his imagination, with sufficient practice, will be able accurately to predict future events. Don't expect too much too soon. I have not only had the characters of persons accurately described, but even their hidden physical marks. Education has little to do with this faculty.

In conclusion: it should take about six months to create a satisfactory pack of cards, and another six months to gain the necessary facility by practice. There is no limit to what may be predicted, using special packs.

Finally, scientists will never prove or disprove anything relating to 'foretelling the future'; it is a work for great artists. But science may subsequently confirm more fully what the artists have already discovered. Note well: all the indications essential for the Psychic Knowledge necessary for developing this specialized ability are given in The Logomachy.

SIXTH FORMULA:
Metamorphoses by "Death Posture"

Powers of visualization, self-discipline and concentration are the qualities necessary. All magical practice, to be effective, needs great courage.

By means of the Death Posture, total transportation of consciousness into the sex-centre occurs. This brings about pure aesthesis and the creation of a new sexuality by autotelic concept:

the subsequent ecstasy is a sublimation.

Because every other sense is brought to nullity by sex-intoxication, it is called the 'Death Posture'. Everything is 'a priori' to the act. The 'a posteriori' illumination reveals the inter-sexual correspondences of all things, and great emotiveness becomes... My desires have made a sentient soul, an obsession, a vampire, an insatiable negress of pendulous breasts and fatted thighs riding me into the abysses of the quadriga sexualis...

SEVENTH FORMULA:
"Transcendental Perspective" as a means of mediumship and anoëtic analgesia–as related to me by the Stoic, Socrates

Many Stoics lived before Zeno and they formulated this sentiment as a practical and ideal behaviourism:

There is in their genesis an hierarchy of form and ideas. Ideas have no status except through forms that are accepted symbols of sentience and are spatially and outwardly self-indulgent. Excarnation of an inspired or superimposed concept may be induced and orientated by 'space-apperception'. The whole body and being must suspire... This total effluxion makes everything reciprocal and becomes a re-orientated sequence of focused nexity. Through this harmonic relation with Ego one becomes the qualitative mediator of the hypothetical or real propensity: any position giving vastness or panorama, and, by abstractive gazing beyond distance, allowing and following the flow of thought until there is an intrusive and more cognate idea. This idea is held and projected into the 'vista'. Nothing innate is permitted to be subtracted from the visualization.

EIGHTH FORMULA:
Formula of Arrivism

AFFIRMATION CREED OF THE ARRIVIST

I am God, and all other gods are my imagery. I gave birth to myself. I am millions of forms excreating; eternal; and nothing exists except through me; yet I am not them—they serve me.

I am inconceivable because I make the conceivable as I so will.

I am beyond Law, for my casualness rationalizes all things to my pleasure.

I am the stranger, ever.

We, the new Arrivists have a lusty heritage from the hierocracy of ancient Egypt, and such great familiars as Lao-Tzû, Pythagoras, Sappho, Socrates, Zeno and others who have substantiated their beliefs (and like them we have been spat on by the ugliest denominators): our great copula is the giving.

'Arrivism' formulates from our integrals: our 'thisness' into 'as if' becoming 'as now'—the intentional becoming extentional; action by spontaneity conforming everything critical and subvertive to itself, which is the mechanism of evoking our 'thisness'.

'As now' has no pendency: things are, because we are always the potential of what we last were. The gospel of the Arrivist is always his own.

HOW TO TRAP AN ARRIVIST FAMILIAR TO EARTH THE ELEMENTAL

The best person to choose would be of the 'arrivist type'—those cocky bastards who seem to obtain all they need whenever they want it. Being intense egocentrics they are mediumistic or susceptible only to silent suggestion... So, look into their eyes and convey to them silently that they are the media for the transit of the obsessing elemental desired. They act simply as something en rapport between you and the elemental. To make yourself acceptive and fit for obsession–acts of sacrifice and purgation are essential beforehand. Also, the elemental must be named and given an appropriate Sigil.

Query to great arrivism: behold everything in the self. Thou art this and all that exists–but here's the catch–never at one time. Mind is universal and includes; Ego separates. 'That art Thou' never is... always. I was or may become this, and only 'I am' in Ego, often losing self-consciousness. I behold multiplicity in all things, and myself as the interrelating oneness, for whatsoever else I conceive will lead me astray or into 'as if'. The more I get into things, the more I am beyond them, so, the more within the more without. I am everywhere present yet unknown to myself except in Ego. I am a configuration of all the multitudinous compositions and designs of this universe, and, knowing not myself fully, how can I know much of other selves and the Gods? But the man we know is mainly made from his beliefs as he enacts them, for 'being' is a function of the all-remembering Soul. So, believe from your necessities, which alone obtain response and recompense–whether good or evil.

[190]

NINTH & FINAL FORMULA:
The Theurgy of Zos

Believing, like breathing, is inveterate whereas 'faith' is a compulsory acceptance for escape... a commitment to an established thesis—often in conflict with our Ids, beliefs and habits.

I, the resurgence of the Apostate Julian, am now the Iconoclast of Theocrasia, for I would have you create a new Pantheism—different Gods and the Great Innocence.

Theses: On Sorcery

Our entire means of expression (of agreed meanings) is semantical, an ambiguous method, whether conveying ideas, values, facts or fictions, which has ever-variant meanings to the recipient; there are few 'one to one' meanings of words. Therefore, although I may transfer by a short sentence a meaning similar to both of us, I do not so convey it to my subconsciousness—there is conjunctional confusion.

Example: The short sentence 'God is love', would be to the subconsciousness either 'god love', or 'love god'. Therefore, to be understood by the subconsciousness it would have to read as 'God=love', and of course this would have to be believed (on your part) to have meaning: lip avowal here has no value for magical transferences. Moreover, the conveyance of such statements is unnecessary and should be in the form of a question, not an answer.

Symbolized:

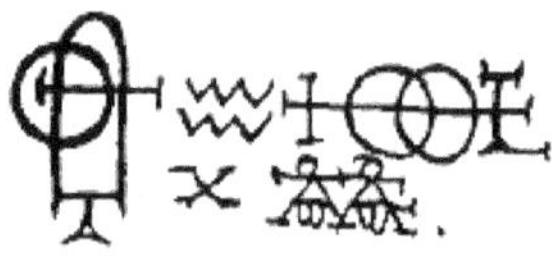

Any fact or fiction has no difficulty in finding relatables as supporting evidence because everything has a 'point of connection' and a period of reality when instantly and simultaneous to time and place. Our difficulty is to re-evoke 'as now': so we accept semblance of (i.e. make-belief, religion or faith) as substitute of real belief (which needs no other reality than its own: what you cannot conceive as yourself is yourself (as another reality).

Abstract or concrete: if you suggest a wish to the thing you desire of, in their own manner, there will be a response: So, if I ask my mind in an appropriate manner for a definition of 'consciousness' I shall receive a true answer, although I may not be able to translate it: semantics are either remiss or insufficient to render the sequence of phonographs, but (without understanding) I would receive an emotional impact, like from a significant passage of music (of Bach or Mozart) thus inspire a kind of semantic rendering. (As true as possible.)

Magic: Belief conjures the Will, becomes the courage, taking its own moral or physical colour. Desire seeks all essential affixes–the only necessity is sincerity.

Importance lies in things 'as now'. Flesh exists to be exploited. It is in all things and all things will be through it. All emanations are through the flesh and nothing has reality for us without it. The Soul is ever unknowable because we can only realize by finite form in Time-Space. So, whatever you attribute to the inconceivable is your Ego, as conceived. The mind and its great thought-stream determines everything and permits all things conceivable as possible. This thought-stream refracts illations both from the Soul and from ourselves into our time-sense–images and symbols which inspire us from the inter-relatabilities, and our reactions form our future destiny of good and evil with thought the nexus to all things past and becoming. Whether the gods created us or we created them is of no import except as an expedient.

Magic is now a quasi-charlatanism seeking victims: magicians have become coprophagists having the most corrupt collection of gleanings and remnants ever given that name. Too long ago its principles were lost, scattered or vulgarized, the symbols losing parallelism and truth. The doctrine lost pageantry, and the rituals became haphazard–the thing itself without inner meaning. As now, Magic adopts an erotic egocentricism as secret meaning, hence there are no Magicians with any simple thesis of the great inner Truth–only a rag-bag remains of this 'wonder' cult. But, one cannot dismiss modern magicians so easily. Yes and no, there is something in most things and little enough in much, if any. Ability to enact is the denominator of our Truth. All parasitical longing seeks flesh to feed on... whether by magic or otherwise.

The deliberate transference of a desire by symbols and sigils with their meanings to the subconsciousness, thus sublating them from the conscious, is a magical act. It works on the thesis that the subconscious is 'all knowing, all memory', and, being universal can 'tap' any source of knowledge. The veriest moron, even, may have dreams as wonderful as those of a genius, whatever their difference of level. Dreams are a 'mental conation', unrecognized as perfect artistry. They prove the creative power of the subconsciousness. Our own degree of ability as a 'personal equation' derives from it, for, genius or not, all difficulties are of expressing adequately our own ethos of inherent ability. By this method of asking, and by the manner of its own showing the subconsciousness will give back all that is necessary for acquiring conative powers. Don't run away with the idea that you can do it first time, or so ride a wild horse! Great belief is essential and it is 'built up' by recollection and endeavour.

A desire for a particular thing appears as conscious requirement and, whatever the difficulties, with sufficient determination you will obtain it: there is no apparent need for magic. The premise is usually weak because of false values. Thus, acquiring a book on sorcery does not make one a magician. The essential abstract requirement is aptitude. Hence all the occult books in the world may give you little knowledge, except as a parrot, and, as more often happens, the ability to do less. The acquired book may help as evocative, so obtain it by all means; by transference of the larger fundamental need for occult knowledge, subconscious mind will in its own way give back all that is necessary to develop your conative ability.

"I am in and of all things..." to a lesser or greater degree, including my own blockheadedness. All thoughts, beliefs, actions are as mine, and this does not imply any equality, superiority or inferiority in my relationships. These levels are rendered different by other differences, for I have discovered the by-passing of generalities—the way of differentiation, not by revolt, submission, resignation, or any such chicanery or bargaining, but by the efferent acceptance of all things. I have opened the pores of my being to breathe freely, and my stomach has no greed to possess of others. Reality, truth, life, are all around us and in us. One cannot escape life. To turn one's back is merely to face it; to close the eyes—the image is retained; the thought, or something more ominous, is ever present. Sleep has many depths and death is but a 'reparative becoming', for we are of eternity in time. Therefore, be willing to pay in the giving and taking without argument, and for him who cheats there is ultimate repayment, for where the morality of exchange ends, business would begin. Sin, however disguised or legalized is sin against self as much as against others. Thus emanates our great inferiority, the down-stepping to the point at which the predator must repay and incarnate as...?—as he deserves.

Why is the subconsciousness always cryptically symbolic and mainly manifests in sleep? As usual, there is more than one answer: 1) Why do the stars only show at night? And, 'hold your hand in front of your face and you cannot see the Sun', i.e., our foreconsciousness is mainly from outside and therefore precludes inner vision. 2) The subconsciousness discloses slowly and latently, because by our limitations we can realize only so much at any 'one time'. 3) Any full disclosure and the whole need and purpose of existence would be unnecessary. And there are other reasons. What we observe from 'outside' becomes memory, enters the subconsciousness and merges with other and older impressions. So, one function of the subconsciousness is to unify these superimposed impressions using the language of parallel symbology and to represent them as simile, not as arbitrary configuration [words illegible in original text]. There is no censor except our own 'outside moral bias'. We do not understand such simple amoral language–

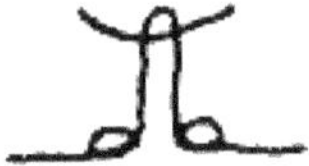

...we make our own filth. Nothing in the subconscious is any more indecent than anything else.

Whether our contacts are psychic or physical they are real, and fear or hope of them determines our way.

With sufficient desire and belief reversion to anoësis may be a means of transforming our physical energy into psychic potency.

Although we cannot know instantly or entirely the contents and processes of the subconsciousness, we can evoke it, and by that act in a measure control it as required, for it will again respond directly to our will. How so? Here is the workable supposition: Truth is not essential to belief, as it always contains sufficient for us to make our truth, for if you believe a thing or idea is true, then it will become as truth for you. Therefore, if we deliberately attach belief to the meaning we give to a sign or symbol, then when we question that sign in our own way, via the subconsciousness, it will answer truthfully.

Illustration: quite arbitrarily I predetermine that if I 'slip on the kerb' it will mean 'this' or 'that' will happen, and it becomes so. Apart from such 'omens' there are many other techniques for evoking my good and evil. "What can I give unto Thee, Thou all-giver? I am blind to Thy gifts and would rather steal from men. Let my belief in Thee be an undistorting matrix of my wish in Thee, and so give the basis of my new reality."

Experiments in Occult Phenomena

Giving my experiences, I do not assert that others will have the equivalent in their practice. Only when the mind is poised in correct juxta-position to the para-normal object is it receptive and able to substantiate. The qualities neces-sary are mainly unknown, and any formula for such is guess-work. We all have some degree of aptitude in some direction, and this is the best guide. Many experiences I cannot reproduce and in some cases even re-vision. These are the most impressive—as if they had been deliberately blotted from my memory, only a vague impres-sion remains. For many years I made every test I could apply to my experiments: "What is unlivable is unbelievable; truth shall be within this limit", was my springboard.

Telepathy I left alone as having been sufficiently proved by involuntary/spontaneous evidence and by deliberate tests.

My experiences at séances were abortive. If giving some evidence of survival, it was of inferior parts of the 'self' still automatically active but not intelligent. Messages were puerile and only of commonplaces already known to me—meaning little except that under certain conditions simple known facts can be transmitted from enquirer to medium and back again. My impression was that many [mediums] had experienced phenomena but that they had no control over them, and in trying to relive [the experience] and to convince others they resorted to fraud.

People do survive death but not in the way they desire to believe. Contact would be as difficult as [with a person a]sleep. My first tests were with prediction; these at least dealt with the future, which precluded faking. My ventures into Astrology, Palmistry, etc., proved their capabilities—and their drawbacks. I found prediction by playing-cards the most resilient and extendible, indeed, almost unlimited in scope and remarkably accurate, and so it became my final choice and convinced me of its possibility for telling anyone's future.

Neither natural aptitude nor much learning is necessary if we begin correctly. Prognostication by cards can be proved beyond question—and demonstrated under almost any conditions, with a person of ability, in its advanced forms. I set no limits whatever. I believe it is possible to forecast the kind of life after death and the nature of one's fresh becomings. I have gone to great lengths and could prove much more than mediums, clairvoyants or clairaudients. In a long predetermined test with a friend (Desmond Coke) I described unknown people in psychical and other detail of such nature as could only be known to the persons concerned, in addition to future events relating to them. The enquirer had no contact with me or the cards, an essential part of this test. Another test by a famous surgeon who asked me to foretell by the cards what he was thinking at a given time: I was warned it would be something unusual and difficult. In a few minutes I gave him the correct answer. Afterwards I showed him how the 'oracle' worked, and he himself was able to perform a similar feat. He was so impressed that he bought my pack of cards at my own price. This has happened more than once.

On another occasion, I carried out a successful series of tests with cards at R. H. Benson's house at Buckingford. These included 'Rain making' and the materialisation of a Traditional Ghost. I mention these experiments to show the capabilities of the medium. 'Cards' may also be used for formulating the will, casting spells, mathematic numerology and, with inventiveness, many other forms of demonstrating the occult powers. I was taught quite early by the greatest 'witch' of recent years.

COMPLETE THESIS AND RITUAL OF MAGICAL TRANSITIVITY

Propositional

That man is a complex of appetites seeking satisfaction–imperative–either 'copulatio or suppositio' (or both).

That by certain arbitrary and deliberate acts he can synchronize desire and event 'as now', i.e., as though arbiter.

That any desire, sufficiently dynamic, compressed into a single wish or belief (as 'question-request'), if arabesquely formulated, will fulfil its evolution expediently and return its conative possibility.

Transference from the conscious to the subconscious *is* automatic when [the wish is] suppressed and sublated by symbols, sigils or glyphs understood either personally or universally. Man is a ratio of his experience, but the subconsciousness is all-knowing (limit unknown).

The mind grants limitless power (will), only measured against belief, and indifferent re: 'quo animo'.

Familiarity breeds all things, including Gods, and Virus, the rare compathy or the commonplace: either we are 'arrivists' or recidivists.

Anyone is capable of anything (will plus belief is ability) if they themselves create the opportune moment and incentive. Heaven gives no genius to disbelievers and no vengeance worse than the body denied.

The terrain between pure Ego (mediator) and ego empirical (conative) is the formative, amalgamative and rationalizing domain which reveals by symbols and metaphor only, and which answers only by such presentation, i.e., a problem, a cryptograph and picturesque arabesques. Hence:

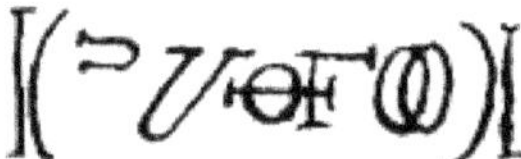

Such a question is answered at once (as near as). But written as an absurd succession of corrupt semantics, thus: "What is truth?", is never answered. The original relation of shapes, sounds and meaning is lost–tortuosities–ambiguously dissipating. Other factors are scattered in the text (q.v.) as given.

Although only one desire is expressed (No. 1, supra), with little alteration it would fit many others. The change is in the Wish, the Familiar employed, and appropriate ritual modifications. Three other alternatives are suggested, the four being classified:

No. 1: Desire for Truth expressed as a question in word-symbols thus:

("What is consciousness?")

Sigillated thus:

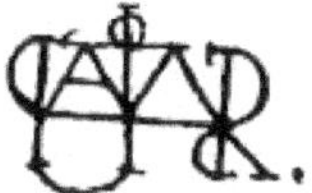

No. 2: Desire for Pleasure. Request to re-
alize Ideal tactually: "I desire a large-bottomed
woman for social congress." As word-symbols:

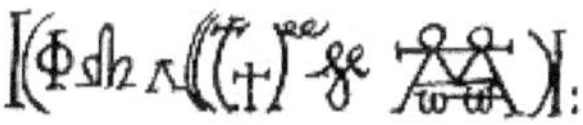

As sigil:

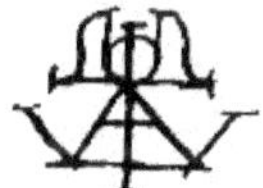

No. 3. Desire for unique experience ex-
pressed as: "I desire intercourse with a vampire".
Word-symbols:

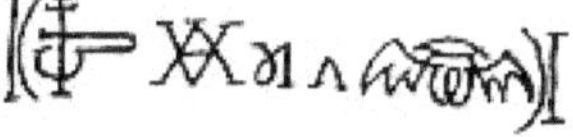

Sigil:

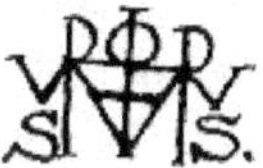

No. 4: Altruistic desire, as: "I wish the death of Stalin".

Word-Symbols thus:

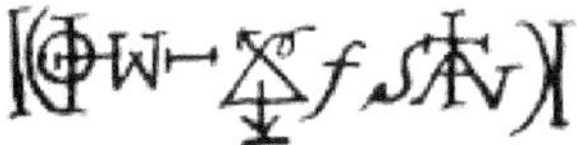

(N.B. Names always given as sigils.)
Sigil:

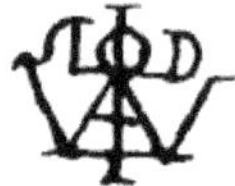

Apart from the above, the rest is symbolic metaphor as an abstract ritual of the thesis, and here the use of spatial and expressive language is justified and gives colour and verisimilitude. Onomatopoeic words should be used.

The ritual opens with an ovation or hymn to Isis—chosen as presiding deity (for personal reasons, though Thoth or Athene would have been more appropriate). Hymn begins:

"O' Glorious Isis, Mother of men, let thy hand reach out and touch my travail...", etc., all of which is expressed by sigils (they should be of one's own composition) followed by the evocation of the familiar or elemental necessary: (1) to act as carrier and bring en rapport subject and object, (2) to pierce the protective aura of the subject, if necessary, (3) to assist the dynamic qualities. The animal chosen should typify the qualities necessary: Tiger = strength, fierceness, etc., or selected from one's own Totem or from face value, i.e., if you look like a horse or a snake, they are your nearest familiars. They are evoked by their secret name which should be inscribed on a strip of parchment, and burnt immediately after calling their name. Except for the name, the evocation is expressed by word-symbols. The familiar chosen is Horus:

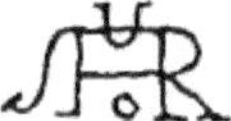

Or an Owl could be used. The operator's stance is entirely 'exercite', his gnosis is within the arcanum symbolized by a geometric form without a parallel, issuing from which is the correspondence between all factors used (as modus operandi). Acts of simulation are essential:

For No. 1, writing the desire on a strip of parchment, enclosing it in an envelope and burning or burying it is sufficient—as symbolizing transference. For No. 4, the tradition of making a wax image of the subject and stabbing same should be followed; it is essential that the operator simulates the pains that will be suffered by the victim. The 'Death Posture' (The Book of Pleasure q.v.) is often depicted:

This symbolizes the positive negation of everything except the wish desired. Previous to the adventure, token sacrifices and abstinences should be made. Some will have difficulties of expression, being neither draughtsmen, scholars or writers: it is sufficient to do your best, however naïvely. The only potent magic now existent is Obeah, practised by ignorant, arrested natives, who know not what they do. But they have this virtue—they believe and perform sufficiently the remnants of a great tradition reaching back to the pure and pristine mind of man.

ARBITRARY TRANSFERENCE: ILLUSTRATION

The technique for materializing our demands is simple for Nature embraces all those who seek individuation, as Nature herself seeks every differentiation:

1) Our desire (for the thing) must be whole-hearted and all else sacrificed to that end.

2) Our belief must be fixed and be-lived, at least 'as if'.

3) Our will (nervous energy) must be secret, and suppressed, to create tension and released only at the psychological moment. At that time gaze into, and beyond, the familiar vista (from hill-top), into The Aeon, the spaciousness beyond your meannesses, corners of reality, borrowed precepts, dogmas and beliefs; until you are in spacious unity. Indraw your breath until your body quivers and then give a mighty suspiration, releasing all your nervous energy into the focal point of your wish; and as your urgent desire merges into the ever-present procreative sea you will feel a tremendous insurge and self-transformation. The Devil himself shall not prevent your 'will' from materializing. In your prayers (media), remember: your Soul is your nearest, and the bringer of all good things. Your God is stone deaf.

Other Fine Titles Available and Forthcoming from Trident Press:

Blood-Soaked Buddha/Hard Earth Pascal by Noah Cicero

it gets cold by jasper avery

Major Diamonds Nights & Knives by Katie Foster

Cactus by Nathaniel Kennon Perkins

Sixty Tattoos I Secretly Gave Myself at Work by Tanner Ballengee

The Silence is the Noise by Bart Schaneman

The Pocket Peter Kropotkin

The Pocket Emma Goldman

The Pocket Aleister Crowley

Propaganda of the Deed: The Pocket Alexander Berkman

The Soul of Man Under Socialism by Oscar Wilde

Los Espiritus by Josh Hyde

America at Play by Mathias Svalina

Western Erotica Ho by Bram Riddlebarger

With a Difference by Nick Gregorio & Francis Daulerio

Order at tridentcafe.com/trident-press